What Bible Sentences Show Us

Kathleen Black

Kitelko Publishing
St. Paul, Minnesota

Kitelko Publishing
1484 Arden View Dr.
St. Paul, MN 55112-1942
Kitelko@comcast.net

Library of Congress Control Number   2009906600

ISBN   978-0-9770834-3-5

Printed and bound in the United States of America
Cover Design: Caitlin L. Johnson
First printing 2009

Acknowledgements

To my husband, Thom Black
With gratitude for his encouragement

Members of the Honors Program of Northwestern College in St. Paul, Minnesota, contributed ideas, examples, and proofreading to this book. Notable among this group have been the following students (in alphabetical order): Stephanie (Hicks) Bell, BriAnn Hoffman, Jacqui Herrmann, Sarah Lysaker, Carrie Noennig, Jennifer Ooms, Catherine Rivard, Claire Thurman, and Katie Waldner. Their enthusiasm for enabling others to read the Bible more effectively has been encouraging. I would like to thank them most sincerely for their contributions.

Kathleen Black, Ph. D.
Northwestern College
St. Paul, Minnesota

Contents

Chapter 1 Introduction to Biblical Sentence Study 1

    Why do we need to study the sentences of the Bible? 1

    Why study English grammar when the original languages were Hebrew and Greek? 1

    What about all the different translations and paraphrases? 1

    What if I never learned grammar when I was in school? 2

Chapter 2 Basic Sentence Elements 3

  IDENTIFYING SUBJECTS AND PREDICATES 3

  IDENTIFYING TYPES OF VERBS 4

    Linking Verbs 4

    Significance of the Linking Verb 5

    Transitive Verbs 6

    Intransitive Verbs 8

  IDENTIFYING ADVERBS 8

  IDENTIFYING ADJECTIVES 8

  SIGNIFICANCE OF THE GRAMMAR BASICS FOR BIBLE SENTENCES 9

Chapter 3 Sentence Varieties 13

  SIGNIFICANCE OF QUESTIONS IN THE BIBLE 13

  SIGNIFICANCE OF INVERTED BIBLE SENTENCES 13

  SIGNIFICANCE OF EXTRAPOSED SENTENCES 15

  SIGNIFICANCE OF PARALLELISM IN THE BIBLE 16

  SIGNIFICANCE OF ELLIPSIS IN BIBLE SENTENCES 18

  OTHER SENTENCES WHICH VIOLATE THE CONVENTIONS 19

  QUESTIONS FOR ANALYZING SENTENCE VARIETIES 20

  SOME PRACTICE 21

Chapter 4 Verbs 23

  SIGNIFICANCE OF VERBS IN BIBLE SENTENCES 23

    Past, Present, and Future 23

    Verb Particles 23

  PROGRESSIVE, PERFECT, AND CONDITIONAL VERBS 23

  IMPERATIVE VERBS: COMMANDS, REQUESTS, OR INSTRUCTION 25

  PASSIVE VERBS 28

    The Divine Passive 29

  EMPHATIC VERBS 30

  QUESTIONS FOR ANALYZING VERBS IN BIBLE SENTENCES 30

  SOME PRACTICE 31

Chapter 5 Noun Structures 33

  PRONOUNS IN SCRIPTURE 33

    Identifying Pronouns 33

    Significance of Pronouns in Bible Sentences 33

  DETERMINERS WITH NOUNS IN SCRIPTURE 34

    Identifying Determiners 34

    Significance of Determiners with Nouns in Bible Sentences 34

  PREDICATE NOMINATIVES IN SCRIPTURE 35

    Identifying Predicate Nominatives 35

    Significance of Predicate Nominatives in Bible Sentences 36

Noun Appositives in Scripture...37
    Identifying Noun Appositives...37
    Significance of Noun Appositives in Bible Sentences.......................................38
    Intensifiers...40
Questions for Analyzing Noun Structures...41
Some Practice...41

Chapter 6 Connecting Elements **43**
Significance of Pro-forms in Bible Sentences 43
    Pronouns..43
    Other Pro-forms...45
Significance of Conjunctions in Bible Sentences..45
    Coordinating Conjunctions 45
    Subordinating Conjunctions 48
    Adverbial Conjunctions..49
Significance of Whole-Sentence Modifiers in Bible Sentences.................................50
    Absolutes 50
    Nouns of Direct Address 51
    Other Sentence Introducers 52
Questions for Analyzing Connecting Elements...52
Some Practice...53

Chapter 7 Adjectival Structures **55**
Identifying Predicate Adjectives 55
    Simple Predicate Adjectives..55
    Expanded Predicate Adjectives...56
    Similes..57
    Other Types of Predicate Adjectives 58
Identifying Adjectival Modifiers 58
    Simple and Expanded Adjectives...58
    Adjectival Appositives..59
    Prepositional Phrases 59
    Infinitive Phrases 60
    Relative Clauses 60
    Participial Phrases..61
Significance of Adjectives in Bible Sentences..62
    To Add Descriptive Detail...62
    To Give Important Explanation and Instruction 62
Questions for Analyzing Adjectival Structures..63
Some Practice...63

Chapter 8 Adjectival Clauses and Phrases **65**
Analyzing Adjectival Clauses and Phrases 65
    What is the Head?..65
    Is the Modifier Restrictive or Nonrestrictive? 66
Restrictive Modifiers 66
Nonrestrictive Modifiers 67
Significance of Adjectival Clauses and Phrases in Scripture 69
    To Clarify Identification...69
    To Describe Abstract Terms...70

To Explain and Teach 70

To Describe God 71

QUESTIONS FOR ANALYZING ADJECTIVAL CLAUSES AND PHRASES 73

SOME PRACTICE 73

Chapter 9 Adverbial Structures **75**

QUESTIONS THAT ADVERBS ANSWER 75

RECOGNIZING ADVERBS 76

SIGNIFICANCE OF ADVERBS IN BIBLE SENTENCES 80

To Understand the Details of the Narrative 80

To Understand Metaphors or Abstract Concepts 81

To Give Context for the Application 81

To Reveal Important Theological Truths 85

QUESTIONS FOR ANALYZING ADVERBS 86

SOME PRACTICE 86

Chapter 10 Putting It All Together **89**

PHRASE ANALYSIS OF SPECIFIC PASSAGES 89

COMPARISON BETWEEN DIFFERENT VERSIONS 104

WHERE DO WE GO FROM HERE? 106

Index **107**

Chapter 1
Introduction to Biblical Sentence Study

Why do we need to study the sentences of the Bible?

All of us, even those of us who have never gone to seminary or become full-time Christian workers, are called to study the Word of God. Paul reminds us in 2 Timothy 3:16 – 17 that *"all Scripture is inspired by God and profitable for teaching, for reproof, for correction, for training in righteousness; that the man of God may be adequate, equipped for every good work."* (NASB). This book strives to provide you with the grammatical tools to understand the Word of God more easily and apply it in the manner that Paul instructs.

Basic method of Bible study is to follow these three steps.
- What does it say?
- What does it mean?
- How does it apply to me?

This book is based on the assumption that understanding the grammar of sentences in the Bible will give us better understanding of what it says. Grammar also gives us implications for what the Bible means. From that point, a student of Scripture could use grammar to ponder the application of the messages.

For example, understanding the sentence structure can alert us to the use of transitions. John 3:16 begins with "for," which signals that the previous verse includes additional information which may be essential to its understanding. Understanding grammar allows us to perceive connections and the details of events, provides clearer definitions, emphasizes different elements, and even clarifies theology.

While this book encourages a closer look at individual sentences, we always need to study the context of the Bible sentences. Bible sentences do not exist in isolation.

Why study English grammar when the original languages were Hebrew and Greek?

Actually, the answer to that question is simply that most of us don't know Hebrew and Greek. Yet, we still want to study the Bible and get insights from the Word. We need to trust that the translators have accurately rendered the sentences.

This book is examining English grammar, specifically the Edited American English system.

What about all the different translations and paraphrases?

You are probably aware of the many versions of the Bible that exist in English. Some translations claim to be more literal than the others are, as close as possible to the form of the original text from which they are taken, in both words and grammar. Other translations attempt to keep the meaning that the author intended but use idioms and syntax that are more modern. Finally, there are paraphrases, which, in effect, try to convey the interpretation or meaning that the translators think the passage has.

Rather than advocate one version over the others, this book outlines methods as tools that can be used on any of the English translations. Each verse will indicate which version is being used, referencing the abbreviations listed below. It is your choice as to which version of the Bible you choose to study.

The versions used in this book are below with their abbreviations:

- American Standard Version (ASV)
- Amplified Bible (Amplified)
- Contemporary English Version (CEV)
- English Standard Version (ESV)
- Holman Christian Standard Bible (HCSB)
- King James Version (KJV)
- New American Standard Bible (NASB)
- New Century Version (NCV)
- New International Version (NIV)
- New King James Version (NKJV)
- New Living Translation (NLT)
- Revised Standard Version (RSV)
- The Message (The Message)

The syntax (sentence structure) in a paraphrase will be closest to modern Edited American English, but then you are dependent upon the understanding and correct paraphrasing of someone else for your study of Scripture. If you choose a more literal translation rather than a paraphrase, you are more likely to need the grammatical concepts in this book. In a more literal translation, the sentence structure is more likely to vary from that of modern English. Because the translators wanted to follow as closely as possible the structure of the original language, you might need to "untangle" some of the sentences. Particularly with the aid of this book, you need not be discouraged by a literal translation, however, and you can apply the grammatical analysis to any version of the Bible. Even a study of a paraphrase of Scripture can benefit from knowledge of grammar.

The bottom line is that it is a good idea to check more than one version when you do Bible study. There could be other grammatical structures, but often this will not significantly affect meaning. You might find that reading another version in addition to your favorite one will help you understand more completely.

For a further discussion of this issue, please refer to the comparisons of different versions in Chapter 10.

What if I never learned grammar when I was in school?
A few basic grammatical terms are used in the book, but every effort has been made to avoid the technicalities in order to get at the importance. We are using only enough grammatical detail so that we can discover greater meaning. Terms and concepts are explained using biblical passages in order to make the impact clear.

Chapter 2
Basic Sentence Elements

If you have done previous Bible study, you have probably noticed that many Bible sentences (particularly those in Paul's letters!) are long and complicated. We can get lost in the language and lose the meaning. It is important that we start by finding the sentence basics: the subject, the verb, and, if there is one, the direct object or predicate nominative or predicate adjective. We cannot examine any subtleties of meaning in the sentence until we find the main parts.

For purposes of Bible study, the basic sentence elements of English can best be categorized by function, rather than by structure. Merely picking out parts of speech so that we can correctly label them will not help us understand the Bible. Instead, we are trying to determine how a word or group of words <u>functions</u> within a sentence. Knowing the function will aid us in determining the meaning of the sentence.

The four most basic categories of grammatical function in English are **verbs**, **nominals** (nouns and other noun-like structures), **adjectives**, and **adverbs**. The easiest way to recognize these basic functions is to understand the basic sentence patterns in English. Each of the patterns has a subject. We can identify basic sentence patterns by looking at the predicate: the type of verb in the sentence and what follows the verb.

Identifying Subjects and Predicates

Before we can discuss the significance of subjects in Scripture sentences, we need to be able to identify the subjects. The subject of a sentence is always a type of nominal (noun or noun-like structure). In an English sentence, the subject will usually precede the predicate. Decoding a sentence begins with identifying the subject, the "who" or "what" in the sentence about which something is being said. When identifying the subject, ask yourself, "<u>who/what is acting or being acted on</u> in this sentence?" The subject of a sentence is sometimes only one word and other times may be an entire phrase or multiple phrases. Be sure to identify the entire subject, not just part of it.

In this example, the subject of the sentence is just one word.
- *David ran and stood over him.* (1 Samuel 17:51, HSCB).

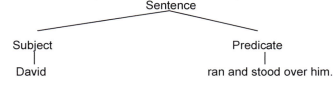

In this next example, the subject of the sentence is many words.
- *Not only so, but **we ourselves, who have the firstfruits of the Spirit,** groan inwardly as we wait eagerly for our adoption as sons, the redemption of our bodies.* (Romans 8:23, NIV).

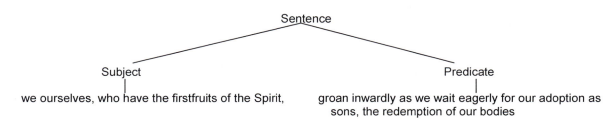

Although in English the subject generally precedes the predicate, sometimes Bible sentences are inverted for style reasons. In this case, the sentence should be mentally "untangled" for meaning. (See Chapter 3 for a further discussion of this concept.)

Merely identifying the subject of a sentence can be important. It allows us to really think about "who/what" is doing the action or "who/what" is being acted upon. In the following examples, the subject is in bold.

- *For **He** chose us in Him, before the foundation of the world, to be holy and blameless in His sight.* (Ephesians 1:4, HCSB). The "he" in this sentence is the subject and refers to God; he is the one doing the action. It is significant in this passage that God chose us and has given us salvation; salvation is not something that we have earned or deserved.
- *Therefore **the Lord** longs to be gracious to you, and therefore **He** waits on high to have compassion on you.* (Isaiah 30:18a, NASB). In this sentence, "the Lord" is doing the acting. He is the one who wants to be gracious and have compassion.

It is also important to identify the entire subject, not just part of it.

- *But now in Christ Jesus **you who once were far away** have been brought near through the blood of Christ.* (Ephesians 2:13, NIV). Identifying the entire subject of this sentence gives greater meaning to this verse. "You who once were far away" refers to the Gentiles who had no hope of salvation until Christ's death and resurrection.
- *Blessed is **she who has believed that what the Lord has said to her will be accomplished**!* (Luke 1:45, NIV). This is an inverted sentence. The full subject is in bold. In this case, the entire subject is important because we can tell that "she" is Mary, and we can infer why she was blessed (because she "believed that what the Lord has said to her will be accomplished"). In this case, identifying the whole subject is important to the meaning.

Identifying Types of Verbs

Linking Verbs

This type of verb indicates a state of being. Many times the linking verb is a word such as *is, was, were, are,* or *am,* but other words can also function as linking verbs if they are indicating a state of being.

Verbs that Can Function as Linking Verbs						
is	be	being	seem	sound	smell	grow
was	are	been	become	look	feel	
were	am	remain	appear	taste	stay	

A linking verb in English is followed by either a noun or noun cluster (called a **predicate nominative**) or by an adjective or adjective cluster (called a **predicate adjective**). The linking verb does what its name suggests. It shows that there is some type of <u>link</u> between the subject and the predicate nominative or predicate adjective. Predicate nominatives rename the subject and predicate adjectives describe the subject. When we see a linking verb in the Bible, we should think about the nature of that link.

In the examples that follow, the linking verb is in bold and the predicate nominative or predicate adjective is underlined.

- *He **is** <u>a shield to those who walk with integrity</u>.* (Proverbs 2:7b, NLT). Think of the linking verb as an equal sign. Here, **he = a shield to those who walk with integrity**.

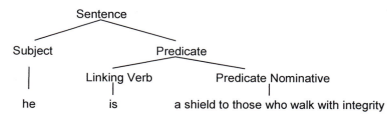

Sometimes there are multiple predicate nominatives. In these cases, it is important to note all of them.

- *I **am** the way, the truth, and the life*. (John 14:6a, NLT).

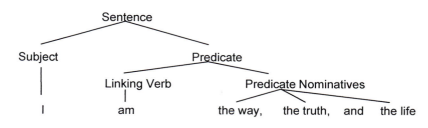

Significance of the Linking Verb

Sometimes the predicate nominative is a definition or identification. Notice that the predicate nominative in the following verses defines or identifies the subject.

- *Eli's two sons, Hophni and Phinehas, **were** the LORD's priests*. (1 Samuel 1:3b, HCSB). Here the predicate nominative ("the Lord's priests") identifies the subject ("Eli's two sons, Hophni and Phinehas").
- *Their teachings **are** but rules taught by men*. (Mark 7:7b, NIV). The predicate nominative ("rules taught by men") defines the subject ("their teachings").
- *For to me, to live **is** Christ, and to die **is** gain*. (Philippians 1:21, NKJV). The predicate nominatives ("Christ" and "gain") define the subjects ("to live" and "to die").

Often a linking verb followed by a predicate nominative creates a metaphor, a type of comparison. In this case, the subject is renamed in a metaphorical fashion. (See Chapter 5 for a further discussion of this concept.)

- *I **am** the true vine, and my Father **is** the gardener....I **am** the vine; you **are** the branches*. (John 15:1, 5a, NIV).
- *I **am** the good shepherd. The good shepherd lays down his life for the sheep*. (John 10:11, ESV). Here, Jesus bestows this name on himself, first asserting his role and then defining it.

A predicate adjective (adjective or adjective cluster) may also follow a linking verb. In these cases, the predicate adjective describes the subject, though perhaps not completely. In the following examples, the linking verb is in bold, and the predicate adjective is underlined.

- *Yet to remain on in the flesh **is** more necessary for your sake*. (Philippians 1:24, NASB).
- *But he said to me, "My grace **is** sufficient for you, for my power is made perfect in weakness."* (2 Corinthians 12:9, ESV).

Sometimes the predicate adjective is a cluster of words starting with the word *like* or *as*. This particular type of predicate adjective is called a simile. Notice in the examples below how much the description in the predicate adjective adds to our understanding of the subject. (For more discussion of similes, see Chapter 7.)

- *Starting a quarrel **is** like a leak in a dam*. (Proverbs 17:14, NCV).

- *A word aptly spoken **is** <u>like apples of gold in settings of silver</u>.* (Proverbs 25:11, NIV).
- *For you **are** <u>like whitewashed tombs—beautiful on the outside but filled on the inside of dead people's bones and all sorts of'impurity.</u>* (Matthew 23:27, NLT).

In the following passage is a series of predicate adjectives. Again, think about the description of the subject that is provided by the predicate adjective.

- *The law of the Lord **is** <u>perfect, reviving the soul</u>. The statutes of the Lord **are** <u>trustworthy, making wise the simple</u>. The precepts of the Lord **are** <u>right, giving joy to the heart</u>. The commands of the Lord **are** <u>radiant, giving light to the eyes</u>. The fear of the Lord **is** <u>pure, enduring forever</u>. The ordinances of the Lord **are** <u>sure and altogether righteous</u>. They **are** <u>more precious than gold, than much pure gold</u>; they **are** <u>sweeter than honey, than honey from the comb</u>.* (Psalm 19:7-10, NIV).

In the next example of linking verbs, the first clause in the sentence has a predicate nominative, and the second clause has a predicate adjective. The first clause is a metaphor (renaming the subject) and the second clause is a simile (describing the subject). These structures are central to the meaning.

- *An excellent wife **is** <u>the crown of her husband</u>, but she who shames him **is** <u>like rottenness in his bones</u>.* (Proverbs 12:4, NASB).

Transitive Verbs

Transitive verbs are called "transitive" because they carry the action to a direct object in the sentence. The direct object is a nominal (noun or noun-like structure) which receives the action of the verb. This type of sentence is common in English. In the following examples, the transitive verb is in bold and the direct object is underlined.

- *A gentle tongue **can break** <u>a bone</u>.* (Proverbs 25:15b, NIV).

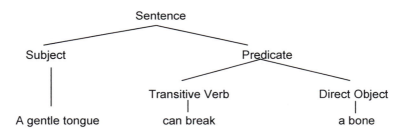

Sentences in the Bible are often compound, and each clause may have a transitive verb with its own direct object.

- *The heavens **declare** <u>the glory of God</u>; and the firmament **shows** <u>His handiwork.</u>* (Psalm 19:1, NKJV).

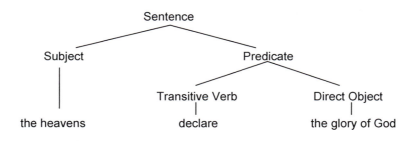

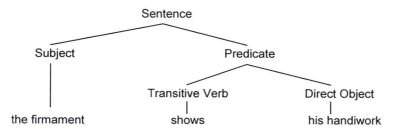

The following Bible sentences all have transitive verbs (in bold) and direct objects (underlined).

- *I **made** <u>you</u> and **will take care of** <u>you</u>. I **will carry** <u>you</u> and **save** <u>you</u>.* (Isaiah 46:4b, CEV).
- *So then each of us **shall give** <u>an account of himself</u> to God.* (Romans 14:12, NKJV).
- *Through him and for his name's sake, we **received** <u>grace and apostleship</u> to **call** <u>people from among all the Gentiles</u> to the obedience that comes from faith.* (Romans 1:5, NIV).
- *He **grants** <u>a treasure of common sense</u> to the honest.... He **guards** <u>the path of the just</u> and **protects** <u>those who are faithful to him</u>.* (Proverbs 2:7-8, NLT).
- *And they came to Bethsaida. And some people **brought** to him <u>a blind man</u> and **begged** <u>him</u> to **touch** <u>him</u>.* (Mark 8:22, ESV).
- *A gracious woman **gains** <u>respect</u>, but ruthless men **gain** <u>only wealth</u>.* (Proverbs 11:16, NLT).
- *A wise son **heeds** <u>his father's instruction</u>.* (Proverbs 13:1a, NKJV).

Sometimes in front of the direct object, we find an indirect object. The indirect object answers the question "to whom" or "for whom." In the verse that follows, the verb is in bold, the direct object is underlined, and the indirect object is in parentheses.

- *The islanders **showed** (us) <u>unusual kindness</u>.* (Acts 28:2a, NIV).

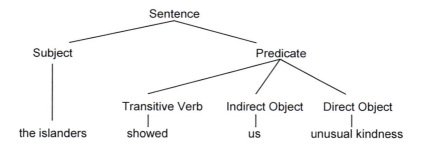

The islanders showed unusual kindness to whom? To us.

In English, we also use a type of direct object that is more complicated, with a word or group of words following the simple direct object to complete the meaning. This type of structure often uses a verb such as *consider*, and one could insert "*to be*" between the simple direct object and the completer. In the following examples, the verb is in bold and the direct object and its completer are underlined.

- *All who are under the yoke of slavery **should consider** <u>their masters worthy of full respect</u>, so that God's name and our teaching may not be slandered.* (1 Timothy 6:1, NIV).

Notice that the words "to be" could be inserted between the simple direct object and its completer: *All who are under the yoke of slavery **should consider** <u>their masters</u> [to be] <u>worthy of full respect</u>, so that God's name and our teaching may not be slandered*

Recognizing this type of sentence and mentally inserting "to be" can help clarify the meaning.

- *Why do You hide Your face and **consider** me [to be] your enemy?* (Job 13:24, HCSB).
- *Do not make any incense with this formula for yourselves; **consider** it [to be] holy to the Lord.* (Exodus 30:37, NIV).
- *Do nothing from rivalry or conceit, but in humility **count** others [to be] more significant than yourselves.* (Philippians 2:3, ESV).
- *Therefore I did not even **think** myself [to be] worthy to come to You. But say the word, and my servant will be healed.* (Luke 7:7, NKJV).
- *"In regard to all the things of which I am accused by the Jews, I **consider** myself [to be] fortunate, King Agrippa, that I am about to make my defense before you today."* (Acts 26:2, NASB).
- *Now therefore do not **hold** him [to be] guiltless, for you are a wise man.* (1 Kings 2:9a, ESV).
- *Yet we **considered** him [to be] stricken by God, smitten by him, and afflicted.* (Isaiah 53:4b, NIV).

Intransitive Verbs

Intransitive verbs do not have a direct object. The action "ends" with the verb. Occasionally, this type of sentence is short.

- *Jesus **wept**.* (John 11:35, NIV).
- *The Lord **reigns**.* (Psalm 93:1, NKJV).
- *The root of the righteous **flourishes**.* (Proverbs 12:12b, NIV).
- *My counsel **shall stand**.* (Isaiah 46:10b, NKJV).
- *So the sun **stood** still and the moon **stopped**.* (Joshua 10:13a, NIV).

However, most often this type of sentence has at least one adverb after the verb.

Identifying Adverbs

Adverbs in English come in a variety of forms (some single words but often groups of words), but they all answer an adverb question such as *how, when, where,* or *why.* If you are trying to find the basic parts of a Bible sentence (subject, verb, predicate adjective, predicate nominative, or direct object), you can ignore the adverb structures. In other words, a group of words answering an adverb question will never be a part of those structures. (We will take a much closer look at adverbs in Chapter 9.)

Adverbs often come after intransitive verbs. In all of the following examples, there is an intransitive verb (in bold) followed by one or more adverb structures (underlined).

- *You **have stooped** to make me great.* (Psalm 18:35c, NCV).
- *When the dew **fell** upon the camp in the night, the manna **fell** with it.* (Numbers 11:9, ESV).
- *After they had heard the king, they **went** on their way, and the star they **had seen** in the east **went** ahead of them until it **stopped** over the place where the child **was**.* (Matthew 2:9, NIV).
- *Wisdom **calls** aloud outside.* (Proverbs 1:20a, NKJV).
- *For just as the sufferings of Christ **flow** over into our lives, so also through Christ our comfort **overflows**.* (2 Corinthians 1:5, NIV).
- *Sharp words **cut** like a sword.* (Proverbs 12:18, CEV).

Identifying Adjectives

Except in the case of predicate adjectives with linking verbs, adjectival structures are attached to nouns to further describe and define the noun. Therefore, these adjectival words or clusters of words should be grouped with nominal structures. Adjectives (except predicate adjectives) help the noun to make up the subject, the predicate nominative, or an object in the sentence. So, as you determine the main parts of the sentence, cluster any adjectives in with the appropriate noun. We will discuss these functions in more detail in later chapters (Chapters 7 and 8). To get started with your study, you need to know only fundamental aspects of adjectives and adverbs.

Significance of the Grammar Basics for Bible Sentences

We began this chapter by stating that we must start our analysis of a Bible sentence by finding the basic parts to get the meaning. This is particularly important if the sentence is long and complicated. The first step is always to find the subject and main parts of the predicate. A few examples will illustrate this point.

Hebrews 10:19-22

- *Therefore, brethren, having boldness to enter the Holiest by the blood of Jesus, by a new and living way which He consecrated for us, through the veil, that is, His flesh, and having a High Priest over the house of God, let us draw near with a true heart in full assurance of faith, having our hearts sprinkled from an evil conscience and our bodies washed with pure water.* (NKJV).

This sentence is an imperative (a request or a command) addressed to "brethren." A series of adjectival structures separates the subject ("brethren") from the transitive verb "let," which is carrying the action to the direct object "(for) us (to) draw near." This sentence is now broken down to its main parts: ***Brethren, let us draw near.***

Recognizing the main thought of this sentence is important because it shows that the adverbs and adjectival structures that form the rest of the sentence are only providing more detail and clarity to this main idea. There are multiple smaller adverbs and adjectives included within the larger adverbial and adjectival structures. (These structures are explained in greater detail in Chapters 7, 8, and 9.)

Adverbial Structures: ***brethren, let us draw near*** – How?
  ➢ *With a true heart in full assurance of faith*
  ➢ *Having our hearts sprinkled from an evil conscience and our bodies washed with pure water*

Adjectival Structures: How are ***brethren*** described?
  ➢ *Having boldness to enter the Holiest by the blood of Jesus, by a new and living way which He consecrated for us, through the veil, that is, his flesh*
  ➢ *Having a High Priest over the house of God*

Ephesians 1:19-21

- *That power is like that working of his mighty strength, which he exerted in Christ when he raised him from the dead and seated him at his right hand in the heavenly realms, far above all rule and authority, power and dominion, and every title that can be given, not only in the present age but also in the one to come.* (NIV).

Although on the surface this sentence appears to be quite long and complicated, it becomes much simpler once the main parts have been identified. By looking at the main elements of the verse, we can identify the sentence pattern and the pieces that hold it together. We have the subject, "that power," followed by the linking verb, "is," and the predicate adjective, "like that working of his mighty strength." The sentence is now broken down into its main parts: ***That power is like that working of his mighty strength***. The rest of the sentence consists of adjectives describing "his mighty strength."

Adjectival Structure: How is ***his mighty strength*** described?

> ➤ *Which he [God] exerted in Christ when he [God] raised him [Christ] from the dead and seated him at his right hand in the heavenly realms.* (Within this adjectival phrase is an adverb that tells us when that mighty strength was used and where it placed the resurrected Jesus in authority.)

Adjectival Structure: How is **the heavenly realms** described?

> ➤ *Far above all rule and authority, power and dominion, and every title that can be given, not only in the present age but also in the one to come.*

Therefore, the mighty strength is the same power that was used to raise Jesus Christ and place him in the proper authority, a power that exists now and forever.

Philippians 2:12-13

- *Therefore, my dear friends, as you have always obeyed—not only in my presence, but now much more in my absence—continue to work out your salvation with fear and trembling, for it is God who works in you to will and to act according to his good purposes.* (NIV).

"My dear friends" is the subject, which is separated from the transitive verb "continue" by an adverb structure. The direct object of the verb is "to work out your salvation." This sentence is now broken down to its main parts: **My dear friends, continue to work out your salvation**. The other word clusters in the sentence are adverbial and provide more detail for the main idea by answering adverb questions. There are other adverbs and adjectives within the larger structures.

Adverbial Structures: **My dear friends, continue to work out your salvation** – How?

> ➤ *as you have always obeyed—not only in my presence, but now much more in my absence*
> ➤ *with fear and trembling*

Adverbial Structure: **My dear friends, continue to work out your salvation** – Why?

> ➤ *For it is God who works in you to will and to act according to his good purposes.*

1 Peter 1:3-5

- *Praise be to the God and Father of our Lord Jesus Christ! In his great mercy he has given us new birth into a living hope through the resurrection of Jesus Christ from the dead, and into an inheritance that can never perish, spoil or fade—kept in heaven for you, who through faith are shielded by God's power until the coming of the salvation that is ready to be revealed in the last time.* (NIV).

The first sentence of this verse presents an immediate puzzle with the first two words and is a great example of how flexible words can be. Words cannot be labeled by themselves but rather must be considered in the context in which they are written or said. "Praise" seems like a verb, but, in this case, it is functioning as the subject of the sentence. The verb has actually been "abbreviated" or elipted (with words left out). The full verb is "be (given)" or "is (given)." (Read more about grammatical ellipsis in Chapter 3.) "To the God and Father of our Lord Jesus Christ" is a prepositional phrase acting as an adverb. It tells us where the praise should go. "Of our Lord Jesus Christ" is another prepositional phrase—an adjective describing "Father." This adjective reinforces whose father is being praised.

Breaking the second sentence into its primary parts helps in understanding. Finding the subject first, we identify "he," which is referring to "the God and Father of our Lord Jesus Christ" from the previous sentence. Second, we find "has given" as the verb phrase. The direct object is "new birth," with an indirect object "us" inserted between the transitive verb and the direct object. This sentence is now broken down to its main parts: **He has given us new birth**.

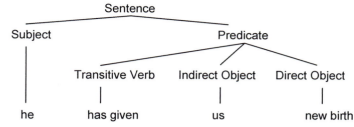

The other parts of the sentence are adverbial and adjectival structures.

Adverbial Structure: ***He has given us new birth*** – Why?

> ➤ *in his great mercy*

Adjectival Structures: How is ***new birth*** described?

> ➤ ***New birth*** *into a living hope through the resurrection of Jesus Christ from the dead*
> ➤ ***New birth*** *into an inheritance that can never perish, spoil or fade*

Adjectival Structure: How is ***an inheritance*** described?

> ➤ It is *kept in heaven for you*

Adjectival Structure: How are ***you*** described?

> ➤ *you, who through faith are shielded by God's power until the coming of the salvation that is ready to be revealed in the last time.*

In later chapters in the book, we will look more closely at structures such as the other structures that are embedded within these long adjectival structures. For now, simply notice that everything that comes after "new birth" plays a role in describing that new birth.

Isaiah 61:1b-3

- *He has sent me to bind up the brokenhearted, to proclaim liberty to captives and freedom to prisoners; to proclaim the favorable year of the LORD and the day of vengeance of our God; to comfort all who mourn, to grant those who mourn in Zion, giving them a garland instead of ashes, the oil of gladness instead of mourning, the mantle of praise instead of a spirit of fainting so they will be called oaks of righteousness, the planting of the LORD, that He may be glorified.* (NASB).

These verses follow the common subject, transitive verb, direct object pattern. "He" is the subject, "has sent" is the verb, and "me" is the direct object. Thus, the sentence is reduced into its main parts: ***He has sent me***. After that structure is a list of adverbs that answer the questions that illustrate the great significance of Isaiah's calling.

Adverbial Structures: ***He has sent me*** – Why? For what purposes?

> ➤ *to bind up the brokenhearted,*
> ➤ *to proclaim liberty to captives and freedom to prisoners;*
> ➤ *to proclaim the favorable year of the LORD and the day of vengeance of our God;*
> ➤ *to comfort all who mourn,*
> ➤ *to grant those who mourn in Zion, giving them a garland instead of ashes, the oil of gladness instead of mourning, the mantle of praise instead of a spirit of fainting so they will be called oaks of righteousness, the planting of the LORD, that He may be glorified.*

Adverbial Structures: ***grant [comfort] to those who mourn in Zion*** – How?

> ➤ *Giving them a garland instead of ashes, the oil of gladness instead of mourning, the mantle of praise instead of a spirit of fainting*

Adverbial Structures: ***bind.., proclaim…, comfort…, grant…*** - Why?

> ➤ *so they will be called oaks of righteousness, the planting of the LORD,*

Adverbial Structures: ***bind.., proclaim…, comfort…, grant…*** - Why?

> ➤ *that He may be glorified*

Philippians 3:4-6

- *If anyone else thinks he has reason for confidence in the flesh, I have more: circumcised on the eighth day, of the people of Israel, of the tribe of Benjamin, a Hebrew of Hebrews; as to the law, a Pharisee; as to zeal, a persecutor of the church; as to righteousness under the law, blameless. (ESV).*

The subject here is "I," referring to Paul. The transitive verb "have" is followed by the direct object "more." This direct object is not complete, however, without the word cluster "reason for confidence in the flesh." This cluster has been ellipted (left out) from the sentence. When it is added back in, the sentence would read as follows: ***I have more [reason for confidence in the flesh]***.

The adverb clause at the front of the sentence shows that Paul is making a comparison. The words "in the flesh" are also an adverb, answering the question *where* the confidence is put. The list that follows the colon would be his reasons for his confidence. They are also ellipted structures with "because" and "I was" or "I am" left out. (For more about ellipsis, see Chapter 3.)

Adverbial Structures: ***I have more reason for confidence in the flesh*** – Why?

> ➤ *circumcised on the eighth day,*
> ➤ *of the people of Israel,*
> ➤ *of the tribe of Benjamin,*
> ➤ *a Hebrew of Hebrews;*
> ➤ *as to the law, a Pharisee;*
> ➤ *as to zeal, a persecutor of the church;*
> ➤ *as to righteousness under the law, blameless*

John 1:1-2

- *In the beginning was the Word, and the Word was with God, and the Word was God. He was in the beginning with God. (ESV).*

The first sentence is actually three separate sentences joined together by conjunctions ("and"). In the first segment, "In the beginning was the Word," the word "was" looks like a linking verb, but it actually is intransitive, because the sentence is out of standard order (called *inversion* and explained in Chapter 3). The standard sentence order is "The Word was in the beginning." "In the beginning" and "with God" (in the second part) are both adverbs, answering the questions *when* the Word was, and *with whom*. Thus, the final construction of the first two sentences, broken down into its main parts, is as follows: ***The Word was***.

Normally, the word "was" (a form of the verb to be) is not used as an intransitive verb. Instead, it is more commonly seen as a linking verb, such as in the third part of the sentence, "the Word was God" where "God" is a predicate nominative renaming "the Word." This unusual use of this word is reminiscent of God's name, I AM. "Am" is also a form of the verb *to be* and is used intransitively here. John is emphasizing the deity of the Word by using a grammatical construction that links the Word with God's own name.

Chapter 3
Sentence Varieties

Not all Bible sentences come in the basic patterns described in Chapter 2. Understanding the varieties of sentences found in the Bible can help our understanding of the meaning and can aid in our interpretation and application. As you read this chapter, notice the significance of each of these sentence varieties.

Significance of Questions in the Bible

In English, we use both "regular" questions and rhetorical questions, and both types appear in Scripture. In a rhetorical question, the answer should be obvious to the reader. Because the answer is expected, the writer uses a rhetorical question to advance the argument or make a point. These examples from Romans show questions that are rhetorical.

- *What shall we say about such wonderful things as these? If God is for us, who can ever be against us*? (Romans 8:31, NLT).
- *We died to our old sinful lives, so how can we continue living with sin*? (Romans 6:2, NCV).
- *What do I imply then? That food offered to idols is anything, or that an idol is anything?* (1 Corinthians 10:19, ESV).

When a "regular" question is being asked, we need to determine the answer.

- *Does God give you his Spirit, and work miracles among you because you observe the law, or because you believe what you heard?* (Galatians 3:5, NIV).

This question states that God gives his spirit and works miracles among the Christians but then asks the question of the cause by giving two possibilities. We will look more closely at adverbs in Chapter 9, but notice that there are two word clusters that begin with "because." They are adverbs of reason (they answer the question "why?"). Therefore, this question asks us which of the causes are correct: "because you observe the law" or "because you believe what you heard." In this case, when we read the verses that surround this one (Galatians 3:1-14), we determine that God gave them the miracles "because [they] believe[d] what [they] heard."

Whether the question is rhetorical or not, a question calls for an answer. For our understanding of Scripture, when we see a question, we should determine the answer.

Significance of Inverted Bible Sentences

"Inverted sentences" is a general term for sentences that do not follow the basic sentence patterns we looked at in Chapter 2. That is, the sentences seem to be scrambled, most likely for stylistic reasons. Bible sentences may be inverted merely to provide variety, but the inversion definitely causes us to slow down as we read. The use of inversion gives a verse emphasis.

The first step to understanding and analyzing inverted sentences for Bible study is to be able to "convert" them mentally into the standard order.

- *Blessed are they that mourn: for they shall be comforted.* (Matthew 5:4, ASV).

The Edited American English form of this sentence would be "*They that mourn are blessed, for they shall be comforted.*"

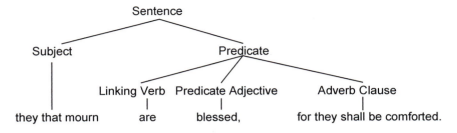

they that mourn   are   blessed,   for they shall be comforted.

Notice how often inverted sentences appear in poetry in the Bible. In fact, these are often called "poetic inversions."

Inverted Bible Sentence	Standard Order
In returning and rest you shall be saved; in quietness and in trust shall be your strength. (Isaiah 30:15, ESV).	You shall be saved in returning and rest; your strength shall be in quietness and in trust.
Moreover by them Your servant is warned, and in keeping them there is great reward. (Psalm 19:11, NKJV).	Moreover, your servant is warned by them, and there is great reward in keeping them.
Better is one day in your courts than a thousand elsewhere. (Psalm 84:10, NIV).	One day in your courts is better than a thousand elsewhere.
Happy is he who does not condemn himself in what he approves. (Romans 14:22b, NASB).	He who does not condemn himself in what he approves is happy.
As a ring of gold in a swine's snout, so is a fair woman that is without discretion. (Proverbs 11:22, ASV).	A fair woman that is without discretion is as a ring of gold in a swine's snout.
Like clouds and wind without rain is a man who boasts of a gift he does not give. (Proverbs 25:14, ESV).	A man who boasts of a gift he does not give is like clouds and wind without rain.
A bruised reed He will not break, and smoking flax He will not quench; (Isaiah 42:3, NKJV).	He will not break a bruised reed, and he will not quench a smoking flax.
Then will all your people be righteous, and they will possess the land forever. (Isaiah 60:21, NIV).	All your people will be righteous then and they will possess the land forever.
Happy are those who hear the joyful call to worship, for they will walk in the light of your presence, LORD. (Psalm 89:15, NLT).	Those who hear the joyful call to worship are happy, for they will walk in the light of your presence, LORD.
As you know, we consider blessed those who have persevered. (James 5:11a, NIV).	We consider those who have persevered [to be] blessed. (Note: This inverted sentence is one of those "*to be*" sentences that we saw in Chapter 2.)

Understanding an inverted sentence is not often difficult; we can generally "unscramble" them into Edited American English. To go beyond understanding to analysis, we look for the emphasis. Remember, the sentence has greater emphasis by its inversion because it takes us longer to read an inverted sentence. Therefore, it is worthwhile to spend more time thinking about the sentence.

In addition, as a general rule, the inversion shifts the emphasis in the sentence to whatever comes first in the sentence. Sometimes this emphasis is possible only with inversion. Notice that the inversion in the following Bible sentences allows the writer to emphasize the adjective at the beginning by placing the word "how" in front.

- *How lonely sits the city that was full of people!* (Lamentations 1:1, ESV).
- *How lovely is your dwelling place, O LORD of Heaven's Armies.* (Psalm 84:1, NLT).

Significance of Extraposed Sentences

The name "extraposed" sounds technical, but actually, in modern Edited American English, we use this type of sentence frequently. In an extraposed sentence, the original subject has been moved to the end of the sentence, and a "placeholder word" (usually *there* or *it*) has been put in the subject position. This placeholder does not have any meaning in the sentence; it is an empty word, merely holding the place of the subject.

- *It is not good for the man to be alone.* (Genesis 2:18, NIV).

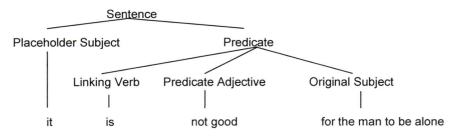

Occasionally putting the extraposed sentence in standard form is easy for us. However, sometimes we write extraposed sentences for style reasons. In the following verse, notice that the "un-extraposed" version sounds unnatural to us.

- *The LORD God said, "**It is not good for the man to be alone**."* (Genesis 2:18a, NIV).
- *The LORD God said, "**For man to be alone is not good**."* (without the empty placeholder *it*).

However, sometimes an extraposed sentence could have been written without the empty placeholder.

- *When her time came to give birth, **there were indeed twins in her womb.*** (Genesis 25:24, HCSB)
- *When her time came to give birth, **indeed twins were in her womb.*** (Without the empty placeholder "there.")

The following chart gives examples of ways in which extraposed sentences can be expressed in standard sentence form. The extraposed sentence is in bold.

Extraposed Sentence	Without the Empty Placeholder Word
*And we answered, "We have an aged father, and **there is a young son born to him in his old age**."* (Genesis 44:20a, NIV).	We have an aged father, and a young son was born to him in his old age.
*For two years now **there has been famine in the land**, and for the next five years **there will not be plowing and reaping**.* (Genesis 45:6, NIV).	For two years now, a famine has been in the land, and for the next five years, no one will be plowing and reaping.
Now **there was no food in all the land**, for the famine was very severe, so that the land of Egypt and the land of Canaan languished by reason of the famine. (Genesis 47:13, ESV).	People in all the land had no food, for the famine was very severe, so that the land of Egypt and the land of Canaan languished because of the famine.
It is easier for a camel to go through the eye of a needle than for a rich person to enter the kingdom of God. (Luke 18:25, NCV).	For a camel to go through the eye of a needle is easier than for a rich man to enter the kingdom of God.

Extraposed Sentence	Without the Empty Placeholder Word
*Why should **it be thought [to be] incredible by you that God raises the dead?*** (Acts 26:8, NKJV).	Why should that God raises the dead be thought [to be] incredible by you?

Because we tend to use extraposed sentences in our normal speech patterns, translators may be using the extraposed form merely to make the passage seem more natural or colloquial to a modern reader. The sentence may also be extraposed for a poetic or dramatic effect.

- *God called the light day, and the darkness He called night and **there was evening** and **there was morning**, one day.* (Genesis 1:5, NASB). This extraposed sentence was clearly written for stylistic reasons, to emphasize the wonder of the creation of "evening" and "morning."

Finally, translators might have chosen the extraposed form to emphasize a particular concept by placing it at the end of the sentence. We should look at the "original subject" at the end of the sentence. The sentence may have been extraposed to add emphasis to this element. This is true in the next three examples. The first part of the sentence creates an evaluation ("It is not good," "it is God's will," and "it is good"), and then we read what "it" is. We get the overall idea first and then can concentrate on the particulars.

- *Then the LORD God said, "**It is not good for the man to be alone**. I will make a helper who is just right for him."* (Genesis 2:18, NLT).
- ***It is God's will that you should be sanctified**.* (1 Thessalonians 4:3, NIV).
- ***It is good not to eat meat or drink wine or do anything that causes your brother to stumble**.* (Romans 14:21, ESV).

The next sentence is extraposed and inverted.

- *Seeing that he became sad, Jesus said, "How **hard** it is **for those who have wealth to enter the kingdom of God!**"* (Luke 18:24 HCSB). This sentence in Edited American English would be "For those who have wealth to enter the kingdom of God is hard." As an inverted sentence, it emphasizes "hard." As an extraposed sentence, as in the examples above, the first part of the sentence makes the evaluation ("how hard it is"), and then we discover what "it" is in the second part of the sentence.

The important aspect of extraposed sentences is two-fold. First, we need to make sure that we are getting the meaning of an extraposed biblical sentence, even if we need to rewrite it mentally, dropping the empty placeholder. In addition, we should examine the sentence to look for the emphasis.

Significance of Parallelism in the Bible

Parallelism is the use of similar grammatical forms for items in a sentence that have the same function. Items in a list are often put in parallel form for stylistic reasons. This parallelism emphasizes those items in a list. In the following examples, the parallel elements are in bold.

- *Wherefore, my beloved brethren, let every man be*
    - ***swift to hear**,*
    - ***slow to speak**,*
    - ***slow to wrath*** (James 1:19, KJV).
- *The Spirit of the Sovereign Lord is upon me, because the Lord has anointed me*
    - ***to preach good news to the poor**.*
    - *He has sent me **to bind up the brokenhearted**,*
    - ***to proclaim freedom for the captives** and **release from darkness for the prisoners**,*
    - ***to proclaim the year of the Lord's favor** and **the day of vengeance of our God**,*

- ○ *to comfort all who mourn, and provide for those who grieve in Zion—*
- ○ *to bestow on them a crown of beauty instead of ashes, the oil of gladness instead of mourning, and a garment of praise instead of a spirit of despair.* (Isaiah 61:1-3, NIV).
- *Praise the Lord, O my soul, and forget not all his benefits—*
  - ○ *who forgives all your sins and heals all your diseases,*
  - ○ *who redeems your life from the pit and crowns you with love and compassion,*
  - ○ *who satisfies your desires with good things so that your youth is renewed like the eagle's.* (Psalm 103:2-5, NIV).
- *Now David assembled at Jerusalem all the leaders of Israel:* **the officers of the tribes** and **the captains of the divisions** who served the king, **the captains over thousands** and **captains over hundreds,** and the **stewards over all the substance and possessions of the king and of his sons,** with the **officials, the valiant men,** and **all the mighty men of valor.** (1 Chronicles 28:1, NKJV).
- **"Ask, and it will be given to you; seek, and you will find; knock, and it will be opened to you.** For **everyone who asks receives,** and **the one who seeks finds,** and **to the one who knocks it will be opened."** (Matthew 7:7-8, ESV).
- Yahweh—Yahweh is a compassionate and gracious God, **slow to anger** and **rich in faithful love and truth, maintaining** faithful love to a thousand generations, **forgiving** wrongdoing, rebellion, and sin. (Exodus 34:6b-7a, HCSB).

Sometimes the entire sentence is in a parallel form to other sentences.

- *The heavens declare the glory of God, and the sky above proclaims his handiwork.* (Psalms 19:1, ESV).
- *When you pass through the waters, I will be with you. When you cross rivers, you will not drown. When you walk through fire, you will not be burned,* nor will the flames hurt you. (Isaiah 43:2, NCV).

Note how the Psalms often use this construction. In the table is Psalm 19:7-10, NLT. The main clause in each sentence mirrors the other main clauses, as demonstrated in the left column. The same thing occurs with the phrases that follow the main clauses, shown in the right column.

The instructions of the LORD are perfect,	*reviving the soul.*
The decrees of the LORD are trustworthy,	*making wise the simple.*
The commandments of the LORD are right,	*bringing joy to the heart.*
The commands of the LORD are clear,	*giving insight for living.*
Reverence for the LORD is pure,	*lasting forever.*
The laws of the LORD are true;	*each one is fair.*
They are more desirable than gold, (Note how the last two lines are different from the others but still parallel with each other.)	*even the finest gold.*
They are sweeter than honey,	*even honey dripping from the comb.*

Parallelism in a sentence will help us focus on the two or more sentence elements that are parallel in form. Noting the parallelism will help us grasp the meaning. The parallelism using the repetition of the word "against" in the following sentence helps emphasize the opposition of our struggle.

- *For our struggle is not **against flesh and blood**, but **against the rulers, against the authorities, against the powers of this dark world** and **against the spiritual forces of evil in the heavenly realms**.* (Ephesians 6:12, NIV).

Also, in some cases, parallelism highlights contrasting elements, such as in the following examples.

- *Better is **a dish of vegetables where love is** than **a fattened ox served with hatred**.* (Proverbs 15:17, NASB).
- ***Anyone who can be trusted in little matters can also be trusted in important matters**. But **anyone who is dishonest in little matters will be dishonest in important matters**.* (Luke 16:10, CEV).
- *Therefore **whoever confesses Me before men**, him **I will also confess before My Father** who is in heaven. But **whoever denies Me before men**, him **I will also deny before My Father** who is in heaven.* (Matthew 10:32-33, NKJV).
- ***Whoever exalts himself will be humbled**, and **whoever humbles himself will be exalted**.* (Matthew 23:12, HCSB).
- *For **whoever desires to save his life will lose it**, but **whoever loses his life for My sake and the gospel's will save it**.* (Mark 8:35, NKJV).
- *No one can serve two masters, for either **he will hate the one and love the other**, or **he will be devoted to the one and despise the other**.* (Matthew 6:24a, ESV).
- ***If you seek him**, you will find him. But **if you forsake him**, he will reject you forever.* (1 Chronicles 28:9b, NLT).

Significance of Ellipsis in Bible Sentences

An ellipsis indicates that something has been left out. We call a sentence ellipted when words are missing, even though they are still grammatically there. To get the meaning, the reader must determine what is missing. In the examples that follow, the omitted words have been inserted in brackets.

Sometimes it is clear that phrases are ellipted to avoid redundancy. The words in bold demonstrate this fact.

- *A wise son brings joy to his father, but a foolish son, **[brings]** heartache to his mother.* (Proverbs 10:1, HCSB).
- *If anyone else thinks he has reason for confidence in the flesh, I have more **[reason for confidence in the flesh]**:* (Philippians 3:4, ESV).
- *If you have any encouragement from being united with Christ, if **[you have]** any comfort from His love, if **[you have]** any fellowship with the Spirit, if **[you have]** any tenderness and compassion, then make my joy complete by being like-minded, having the same love, being one in spirit and purpose.* (Philippians 2:1-2, NIV).
- *Other seeds fell on good soil and produced grain, some **[seeds produced]** a hundredfold **[of grain]**, some **[seeds produced]** sixty**[fold] [of grain]**, **[and]** some **[seeds produced]** thirty**[fold] [of grain]**. He who has ears, let him hear.* (Matthew 13:3b-9, ESV).

In most cases, we can easily understand what has been omitted and can insert the missing words mentally, even if the omitted words are not repeated ones.

- *This is a clear sign to them of their destruction, but of your salvation, and that **[salvation is]** from God.* (Philippians 1:28, ESV).
- *Whether **[the males are]** born in your household or bought with your money, they must be circumcised.* (Genesis 17:13, NIV).
- *A son honors his father, and a servant **[honors]** his master.* (Malachi 1:6, ESV).
- *Do something, whether **[it is]** good or bad!* (Isaiah 41:23, NIV).

- *I have learned the secret of being content in any and every situation, whether **[I am]** well fed or hungry, whether **[I am]** living in plenty or in want.* (Philippians 4:12, NIV).
- *To whom then will you liken God, or what likeness **[will you]** compare with him?* (Isaiah 40:18, ESV).
- *When therefore the Lord knew that the Pharisees had heard that Jesus was making and baptizing more disciples than John **[was making and baptizing]** (although Jesus himself baptized not, but his disciples **[baptized]**), (John 4:1-2, ASV).*

Sometimes in the Bible, we see ellipsis in a sentence that already is inverted or is extraposed.

- *Now for this very reason also, applying all diligence, in your faith supply moral excellence, and in your moral excellence, **[supply]** knowledge, and in your knowledge, **[supply]** self-control, and in your self-control, **[supply]** perseverance, and in your perseverance,**[supply]** godliness, and in your godliness, **[supply]** brotherly kindness, and in your brotherly kindness, **[supply]** love.* (2 Peter 1:5-7, NASB). This verse is also inverted.
- *For as the heavens are higher than the earth, so are my ways higher than your ways, and my thoughts **[are higher]** than your thoughts.* (Isaiah 55:9, KJV). This verse is also inverted.
- *Lebanon is not sufficient for altar fires, nor **[are]** its animals enough for burnt offerings.* (Isaiah 40:16, NIV). This verse is also inverted.
- ***[It is]** Better to live on the corner of a roof than **[to live]** in a house shared with a nagging wife.* (Proverbs 25:24, HCSB). This verse is also extraposed.

Sometimes it is not absolutely clear what words have been omitted.

- *For if Abraham was justified by works, he has something to boast about—**but not before God**.* (Romans 4:2, NASB). The completed verse could be "For if Abraham was justified by works, he has something to boast about—but [he does] not [have anything to boast about] before God." However, it could also be "for If Abraham was justified by works, he has something to boast about—but [he was] not [justified by works] before God." Since Abraham was not justified by works, nor does he have something to boast about before God, both interpretations may be true.

The significance of ellipsis is that it can draw attention or emphasis to parts of the sentence.

- *He has showed you, O man, what is good. And what does the LORD require of you? To act justly and to love mercy and to walk humbly with your God.* (Micah 6:8, NIV). The answer to the question in this verse is ellipted; the full version would be: "[The LORD requires of you] to act justly and to love mercy and to walk humbly with your God." Since that first section is not there, redundancy is avoided and attention is drawn to the action. Furthermore, the word "to" is often ellipted in English in a series, but here the emphasis on the verbs is more prominent with its presence ("to act…to love…to walk…").

Other Sentences which Violate the Conventions

In addition to the sentence varieties that we have already examined, there are sentences in the English versions of the Bible that violate the conventions of Edited American English sentences in other ways. In a few Bible sentences, the direct object, which usually follows the verb in English, comes instead at the beginning of the sentence, and a more general term (usually a pronoun) is used in the traditional direct object position.

In the example that follows, the sentence begins with the direct object followed by a dash. The main part of the sentence then follows the dash, with "them" now substituting for the specific direct object. Notice how putting the direct object first and then using a pronoun later in the direct object position adds emphasis to the importance of the direct object.

- ***Acquitting the guilty and condemning the innocent**—the Lord detests **them** both.* (Proverbs 17:15, NIV). In a normal structure we would say, "The Lord detests both acquitting the guilty and condemning the innocent."

In this second example, the direct object again comes first, with "it" later substituting for the specific direct object. Notice how this gives emphasis to the direct object ("whatever you do, whether in word or deed").

- *And **whatever you do, whether in word or deed**, do **it** all in the name of the Lord Jesus, giving thanks to God the Father through him.* (Colossians 3:17, NIV).

This next sentence starts with part of the direct object, which appears later in its regular position in the form of the word "him." This gives emphasis to the relative clause "who has ears." (See Chapter 7 and 8 for more on relative clauses.)

- ***He who has ears**, let **him** hear.* (Matthew 13:9, ESV).

Another Bible sentence that breaks conventional Edited American English gives the subject first and then repeats the subject with a pronoun. Notice that this method places greater emphasis on the subject.

- *But **a woman who fears the Lord, she** shall be praised.* (Proverbs 31:30b NASB). We would normally say, "a woman who fears the Lord shall be praised." The repetition of the subject (in pronoun form) gives emphasis to the woman and slows us down a bit as we read the verse. We can stop and really think about who is the woman worthy of praise.
- The man said, "**The woman whom You gave to be with me, she** gave me from the tree, and I ate." (Genesis 3:12, NASB). Notice how the repetition of the subject (in pronoun form) gives emphasis to the subject. This emphasis is particularly important since here we see Adam blaming God for his sin. Adam points out that it was God who put Eve in the garden. The subject is emphasized by the repetition since the information included in the subject is important for us to understand what is going on in Adam's statement to God.

Therefore, even if the Bible sentence we are reading violates standard conventions, we should be able to "translate" it into the standard form. The significance of these violations is, however, that the direct object or the specific subject that begins the sentence has been given the emphasis. The pronoun that comes later merely assumes the correct grammatical position in the sentence.

Questions for Analyzing Sentence Varieties

In summary, when trying to understand the significance of sentence varieties in Scripture, ask and answer these questions:

1. If there is a question, determine the answer.
   - If the answer is obvious, then the question is rhetorical. Look to see how the author is using the rhetorical question to make a point.
   - If the question is not rhetorical, then explore the meaning of various answers to the question within the context of that passage.
2. If the sentence is inverted, rearrange it in your head into standard order so that you are sure of the meaning. Think about the reason for the nonstandard order. Check out the emphasis that may be on the beginning of the inverted sentence.
3. If the sentence is extraposed, do the following:

- Make sure that you are getting the meaning of an extraposed biblical sentence, even if you need to rewrite it mentally, dropping the empty placeholder.
- Also, examine the sentence to look for the emphasis. Look especially at the "original subject" that comes at the end of the sentence.

4. Look for parallel elements that clarify the meaning or highlight contrasting elements.
5. Look for any ellipsis. Mentally fill in the missing words to make the meaning clear.
6. Make sure that you notice any other sentence varieties such as those illustrated in the previous section of this chapter. Rephrase the sentence using standard form in order to make sure that you understand it. Notice the emphasis placed on the specific direct object or first mention of the subject.

Some Practice

This chapter examines a variety of different kinds of sentences, including questions, inversion, extraposed sentences, parallelism, ellipsis, and unusual constructions. As always, break the sentence down into its basic parts to understand the meaning, first finding the subject and main parts of the predicate. The following examples demonstrate analysis with these new sentence constructions.

Daniel 2:21-22

- *And He changes the times and the seasons; He removes kings and raises up kings; He gives wisdom to the wise and knowledge to those who have understanding. He reveals deep and secret things; He knows what is in the darkness, and light dwells with Him. (NKJV).*

This passage is an example of poetic parallelism. Each segment uses the same subject "he," which is followed by one or two transitive verbs and direct objects. The only exception to this pattern is the last statement: "and light dwells with him." Because this phrase breaks from the poetic pattern, it becomes the most important. Further emphasis is placed on this idea because it is placed at the end of the passage.

- *It is He who changes the times and the epochs; He removes kings and establishes kings; He gives wisdom to wise men and knowledge to men of understanding. It is He who reveals the profound and hidden things; He knows what is in the darkness, and the light dwells with Him. (NASB).*

Here we see that the translators of the NASB used almost the same parallel pattern as the translators of the NKJV Bible. The difference in the NASB is that the beginnings of both sentences are extraposed so that they read "it is he." This extraposition is meant to emphasize the pronoun "he," stressing that God alone has ultimate authority over all things.

2 Kings 1:6

- *They said to him, "A man came up to meet us and said to us, 'Go, return to the king who sent you and say to him, "Thus says the LORD, 'Is it because there is no God in Israel that you are sending to inquire of Baal-zebub, the god of Ekron? Therefore you shall not come down from the bed where you have gone up, but shall surely die.' " "' (NASB).*

This verse has two of the sentence varieties discussed in this chapter.

First, God asks a question, and we must determine if this is a regular question to which we must determine the answer or if this question is rhetorical and was asked to prove a point. Because the Lord himself is asking whether there is God, we can conclude that the question is rhetorical. He is pointing out the audacity that would be necessary to turn to other gods when he, the "I AM," is present in Israel. The answer to his question is *no*.

Second, this verse has two extraposed parts, both in the same sentence that contains the rhetorical question. To see the first extraposed portion, the verse can be taken out of the usual question form: "It is because there is no God in Israel that you are sending to inquire of Baal-zebub, the god of Ekron?" In an extraposed sentence, the original subject, placed at the end when it is extraposed, often is emphasized more than if it were in the standard subject position at the beginning of the sentence. This sentence's extraposed structure emphasizes the fact that they are "sending to inquire of Baal-zebub."

"There is no God in Israel" is the second extraposed part of the verse. It can be rewritten to read, "No God is in Israel." Written this way, the sentence not only sounds awkward, but also takes the emphasis from God's location, which is provided by the extraposed form.

Hosea 2:2-3

- *Bring charges against your mother, bring charges; for she is not My wife, nor am I her Husband! Let her put away her harlotries from her sight, and her adulteries from between her breasts; lest I strip her naked and expose her, as in the day she was born, and make her like a wilderness, and set her like a dry land, and slay her with thirst.* (NKJV).

This verse is paralleled to highlight God's jealousy for the purity of his people and his intense pain at their betrayal. In the second sentence, the repetitive structure of the objects in the list (verb + *her*), combined with the tedious substitution of "and" between the objects in the list, emphasizes the severity with which God views unfaithfulness.

Chapter 4
Verbs

Significance of Verbs in Bible Sentences

Past, Present, and Future

The form of a verb can add to the meaning. For example, it can be quite important whether a Bible sentence has a verb indicating the present, past, or future. This can have important implications.

For example, see the verse that follows.
- *And we also thank God continually because, when you received the word of God, which you heard from us, you accepted it not as the word of men, but as it actually is, the word of God, which is at work in you who believe.* (1 Thessalonians 2:13, NIV).

This verse talks about an event in the past (when they received God's word from Paul, they accepted it as the word of God). However, note that there are two present tenses involved. Those who sent the epistle of Thessalonians (Paul, Silvanus, and Timothy) continue to thank God, even though the occurrence was in the past. This provides a model for us. In addition, the present tense at the end of the sentence provides an encouragement and motivation for Christians to accept the Word of God. The word of God is (present tense) at work in those who believe. There is no expiration date on this; the verse does not say, "which is at work in you who believe and live between 1200 and 1700 A.D." God's word is always at work in us, and it is powerful.

Another interesting use of present tense is in Galatians.
- *Does God give you his Spirit and work miracles among you because you observe the law or because you believe what you heard?* (Galatians 3:5, NIV). Notice that the verb is "does" and not "did." God *gives* his Spirit, not *gave* his Spirit as a one-time past event.

Verb Particles

Sometimes in English, two words act together as a single verb; a verb may have been a single word in Hebrew or Greek, but we do not have a single word to convey that meaning in English. We need two words to convey the meaning. The second word is called a **verb particle**. For Bible study, we need to recognize these two-word verbs as one language unit. In the examples below, the two-word units are in bold.
- *How, then, can they **call on** the one they have not believed in?* (Romans 10:14a, NIV).
- *Other seeds fell on rocky ground, where they did not have much soil, and immediately they **sprang up**, since they had no depth of soil, but when the sun rose they were scorched.* (Matthew 13:5-6a, ESV).

Progressive, Perfect, and Conditional Verbs

Past, present, and future tenses tell us to some degree when an event occurs. **Progressive** verbs combine with past, present, and future auxiliary verbs to explain an action that is happening and continuing to happen in the present or to convey the idea of an action in the future or in the past that continues or continued for a while. A form of a "*BE*" verb (*is, are, was, were, be, am, been*) plus the *–ing* form of the verb that follows it gives us the progressive tense. Look at the use of the progressive tense in these verses (marked in bold).

- *But even if I **am being** poured out as a drink offering upon the sacrifice and service of your faith, I rejoice and share my joy with you all.* (Philippians 2:17, NASB). The verb indicates present continuing action. The action (Paul "being poured out as a drink offering upon the sacrifice and service of [their] faith") is continuing at the time of the writing.
- *Now the people of Beth Shemesh **were reaping** their wheat harvest in the valley; and they lifted their eyes and saw the ark, and rejoiced to see it.* (1 Samuel 6:13, NKJV). The action "reaping" was occurring and continued for a period of time during the time the narrative took place. This is a past progressive verb.
- *God has given them a desire to know the future. He does everything just right and on time, but people can never completely understand what he **is doing**.* (Ecclesiastes 3:11, NCV). The present progressive verb indicates present continuing action.
- *Maybe so, but I say it is better to be content with what little you have. Otherwise, you **will** always **be struggling** for more, and that is like chasing the wind.* (Ecclesiastes 4:6, NCV). The auxiliary "will" gives the meaning of future tense in English, but the progressive ("be struggling") tells us that the action will be a continuing one, not a single, future event.
- *We **are not trying** to please men but God, who tests our hearts.* (1 Thessalonians 2:4b, NIV). Because the verb "are trying" is present progressive, we see that this incorporates what we do and are continuing to do. It is a progressive action, and attempting to please God should happen every moment of our lives.
- *I **am telling** the truth in Christ, I **am not lying**, my conscience bearing me witness in the Holy Spirit.* (Romans 9:1, NASB). The present progressive verbs indicate that Paul is telling the truth as a continuous action.

The **perfect** tense, created by putting a form of **HAVE** (*had* for past perfect, *has* and *have* for present perfect) before a form of another verb, suggests when an action or state of being begins and ends. Some examples of this form can be found in the following verses.

- *He **has told** you, O man, what is good; and what does the LORD require of you but to do justice, and to love kindness, and to walk humbly with your God?* (Micah 6:8, ESV). In this verse, the present perfect tense lets us know that God told man at a certain point in time what he requires. The "present" part of the present perfect tense in English tells us that the situation continues. The conditions resulting from the action are still in effect at the present. God continues to require these things as good behavior.
- *O LORD, you **have sent** this storm upon him for your own good reasons.* (Jonah 1:14b, NLT). From this verb phrase, we can see that God sent the storm in the past, but that the condition of the storm was still there at the time in the passage.
- *May the LORD, the God of Israel, under whose wings you **have come** to take refuge, reward you fully for what you **have done**.* (Ruth 2:12, NLT). The use of the present perfect tense signifies Ruth's previous decision, and the situation or condition continues. Ruth is still in the situation resulting from her taking refuge with God.
- *God looked over everything he **had made**; it was so good, so very good!* (Genesis 1:31a, The Message). Using past perfect tense in this verse further reminds us that God's creating produced concrete, instant results. Because it is past perfect, rather than present perfect, the action (making) was over, and God "looked over everything."
- *For though I am free from all men, I **have made** myself a servant to all, that I might win the more.* (1 Corinthians 9:19, NKJV). The verb "have made" is a present perfect, indicating that this is an action that Paul started in the past, and the condition of his servanthood still continues to exist.

In Edited American English, we use **conditional** verb phrases to communicate the possibility of an action or the ability to complete an action, rather than communicating that the action actually occurred or is occurring. Auxiliary verbs such as *might, should, could, can, must, will,* and *shall* come before the main verb and alter the meaning of the verb in a sentence. That is the reason we call these verbs "conditional"; they put conditions of some sort on the verb. The main concept to remember when studying sentences that contain the conditional verb tense is that the action has not yet happened and has a condition attached to it. For example, the action might not happen at all, even if it should happen. Consider the implications of this in the following examples.

- *These have come so that your faith—of greater worth than gold, which perishes even though refined by fire—**may be proved** genuine and **may result** in praise, glory and honor when Jesus Christ is revealed.* (1 Peter 1:7, NIV). The verbs are conditional, with the use of "may." In this verse, your faith is not guaranteed to prove genuine or result in praise, glory and honor; it is a possibility. The context of the verse shows us that "these" refers to the trials Christians were enduring.

- *God did this so that men **would seek** him and perhaps [**would**] **reach out** for him and [**would**] **find** him, though he is not far from each one of us.* (Acts 17:27, NIV). The "would" here applies to the verbs "seek," "reach out," and "find." We have three conditional verbs. Notice the difference of condition using "would" rather than "will." Men might not seek and reach out for God, but God has made it possible.

- *For though I am free from all men, I have made myself a servant to all, that I **might win** the more.* (1 Corinthians 9:19, NKJV). This verse was included under the perfect verb examples, but it also belongs here because the verb "might win" is conditional, indicating that this is a possibility dependent upon Paul's being a servant to all men.

- *Put on the whole armor of God, that you **may be** able to stand against the schemes of the devil.* (Ephesians 6:11, ESV). The use of the word "may" indicates that there are conditions that must be fulfilled before standing against the devil, namely, putting on the whole armor of God.

- *Each of you **should look** not only to your own interests, but also to the interests of others.* (Philippians 2:4, NIV). Notice the conditional word "should" in this conditional verb. We ought not to ignore the condition attached with the word "should." Paul was addressing the church of Philippi, but this can also be extended to today's Christians.

- *Above all, you **must live** as citizens of heaven, conducting yourselves in a manner worthy of the Good News about Christ.* (Philippians 1:27a, NLT). Using the conditional auxiliary verbs "should" or "must" give the action the force of a command. That we ought to conduct ourselves in a manner worthy of the Good News about Christ is particularly important, indicated through the words "above all." (See Chapter 6 for a discussion of phrases such this, called "whole-sentence modifiers.")

Imperative Verbs: Commands, Requests, or Instruction

One particular verb form to watch for is the imperative. We use this verb form for commands or requests. An imperative sentence, such as "Listen to me," seems to be missing a subject and generally begins with the imperative verb. An implied "you" is the subject in a command. These imperatives are found throughout the Bible. Notice that a command can be simply "be" followed by an adjective.

- ***Do not be overcome** by evil, but **overcome** evil with good.* (Romans 12:21, NIV).

- *So **be careful** to do what the LORD your God has commanded you; **do not turn aside** to the right or to the left. **Walk** in all the way that the LORD your God has commanded you, so that you may live and prosper and prolong your days in the land that you will possess.* (Deuteronomy 5:32-33, NIV).

- *Be strong and of good courage, for to this people you shall divide as an inheritance the land which I swore to their fathers to give them. Only be strong and very courageous, that you may observe to do according to all the law which Moses My servant commanded you; do not turn from it to the right hand or to the left, that you may prosper wherever you go.* (Joshua 1:6-7, NKJV).
- *Open your mouth and taste, open your eyes and see—how good GOD is.* (Psalm 34:8, The Message).
- *Trust the Lord with all your heart, and don't depend on your own understanding.* (Proverbs 3:5, NCV).
- *Flee for your lives! Don't look back, and don't stop anywhere in the plain! Flee to the mountains or you will be swept away!* (Genesis 19:17, NIV).
- *Humble yourselves, therefore, under the mighty hand of God so that at the proper time he may exalt you, casting all your anxieties on him, because he cares for you. Be sober-minded; be watchful.* (1 Peter 5:6-8a, ESV).
- *Learn to appreciate and give dignity to your body, not abusing it, as is so common among those who know nothing of God.* (1 Thessalonians 4:4-5, The Message).
- *"Go and bring your husband."* (John 4:16b, CEV).
- *"Go and prepare the Passover for us, that we may eat it."* (Luke 22:8b, NASB).
- *Devote yourselves to prayer, keeping alert in it with an attitude of thanksgiving.* (Colossians 4:2, NASB).
- *"Sing and rejoice, O daughter of Zion! For behold, I am coming and I will dwell in your midst,"* says the LORD. (Zechariah 2:10, NKJV).
- *"Give back to Caesar the things that are Caesar's and to God the things that are God's."* (Luke 20:25b, HCSB). Jesus is responding to questions raised about taxes, bringing a heavenly perspective into these issues.

The first important aspect of interpreting an imperative is to <u>determine by whom and to whom the instruction is being given</u>.

- *"Get up! Hurry and take the child and his mother to Egypt! Stay there until I tell you to return, because Herod is looking for the child and wants to kill him."* (Matthew 2:13b, CEV). The angel of the Lord is addressing Joseph.
- *Rejoice in our confident hope. Be patient in trouble, and keep on praying.* (Romans 12:12, NLT). This command was written to Christians in Rome, but we can assume that the command is also meant for us.

Of course, it is particularly important to note God's specific commands. For example, Genesis 1 contains six different times during which God commanded something to be created out of nothing. Jesus commanded the wind and waves to "be still" in Mark 4:39, and there was calm instantly. The demons obeyed when commanded to leave the man in Luke 4:35. All inanimate parts of the universe and even the evil spirits obey God when he commands them. We, of course, must also heed God's commands when they are given to Christians.

- *Go therefore and make disciples of all nations, baptizing them in the name of the Father and of the Son and of the Holy Spirit, teaching them to observe all that I have commanded you.* (Matthew 28:19-20a, ESV). Here the command is given by Jesus to his disciples. We assume that the command applies to us as well. We are called to go to all nations and make disciples by baptizing and teaching the importance of obeying God's commands. The importance of divine imperatives is extremely clear in this verse since obeying commands is a vital element of discipleship.

Sometimes a command from God is expressed in the negative.

- *You **shall not murder**. You **shall not commit** adultery. You **shall not steal**. You **shall not give** false testimony against your neighbor.* (Exodus 20:13-16, NIV).
- ***Don't make** idols for yourselves; **don't set up** an image or a sacred pillar for yourselves, and **don't place** a carved stone in your land that you can bow down to in worship. I am GOD, your God.* (Leviticus 26:1, The Message).
- *And he said to them, "**Take nothing** for your journey, neither a staff, nor a bag, nor bread, nor money; and **do not** even **have** two tunics apiece."* (Luke 9:3, NASB).
- ***Do not tremble** or [**do not**] **be dismayed**, for the LORD your God is with you wherever you go.* (Joshua 1:9b, NASB).

In commands, the subject is not usually stated, but merely implied as "you." Because commands are so important in the Bible, it is essential for us to consider who is included in the "you" when we find a command.

- ***Sing** about his glorious name. **Honor** him with praises.* (Psalm 66:2, CEV). Who should sing about his name and honor him with praises? In this case, we look in the previous verse to see that the implied subject "you" means "all the earth." (See Psalm 66:1).
- ***Rejoice** always, **pray** without ceasing, in everything **give** thanks; for this is the will of God in Christ Jesus for you.* (1 Thessalonians 5:16-18, NKJV). Paul directly gives these commands to the Christians in Thessalonica. The implied subject "you" (which is directly mentioned in verse 18) initially referred to these Christians: however, there is no reason not to infer that God's will for the Thessalonian Christians applies to us as well.
- ***Call** to me and I will answer you and tell you great and unsearchable things you do not know.* (Jeremiah 33:3, NIV). This sounds like a command with a promise that God will answer and tell great and unsearchable things. However, in this verse, God is not speaking directly to us. Rather, the implied "you" here is Jeremiah. (See Jeremiah 33:1-2).

Sometimes the implied subject of a command is debated. In the context of Exodus 20, the Ten Commandments are directed toward Moses and the Israelite nation. Some Christians debate whether the command is also directly toward a more general "God's people."

The second important aspect of interpreting an imperative is to note <u>the context of a command</u> and <u>the conditions (or lack of conditions) that may accompany a command</u>. This is particularly important when we read a command to us from God.

- ***Do not love** the world or the things in the world.* (1 John 2:15, NKJV). This is an example of a command that is negatively stated. If John 3:16 says that *God so loved the world*, how then can we be commanded to do the opposite? We must consider how this love is to be shown. God's love of the world compelled him to sacrifice himself to save it. However, when we are told in 1 John 2:15 to *not love the world*, he is giving us this commandment to keep us from following the ways of the world. Because our love of the world is different from God's love of the world, we need to abandon our desire for the world and trade it for a relationship with God that enables us to love the world rightly. The context is important to understanding the command.
- ***Rejoice** always, **pray** without ceasing, in everything **give** thanks; for this is the will of God in Christ Jesus for you.* (1 Thessalonians 5:16-18, NKJV). Note that there are conditions along with these commands: "always," "without ceasing," and "in everything."
- ***Rejoice** and **be** glad, because you have a great reward waiting for you in heaven.* (Matthew 5:12, NCV). Notice that this verb is not conditional upon previous or present circumstances but is defining an attitude that we are to have based upon a future reward. The context of the

command helps us to understand the command. In this case, God gives us the reason for the command.

- *A new command I give you:* **Love** *one another. As I have loved you, so you must love one another.* (John 13:34, NIV). This command does have a condition ("as I have loved you"). A study of what it means to love as Christ loved his disciples is beyond the scope of this book, but we do need to note that we are being told how to obey this command, to love one another as Christ has loved us. Another important aspect of this command is that it is repeated in the form of a conditional verb ("must love"), which further emphasizes this command's importance, especially since it is repeated throughout the Bible, (Leviticus 19:18, John 15,12, Ephesians 5:2, 1 Thessalonians 4:9, and 1 John 3:11, for example).

It is interesting that sometimes God allows us to make a request of him. By requesting of God, we express our faith that God will act.

- **Restore** *us, O LORD God of hosts!* **Let** *your face shine, that we may be saved!* (Psalm 80:19, ESV).
- *In Your justice,* **rescue** *and* **deliver** *me;* **listen** *closely to me and* **save** *me.* (Psalm 71:2, HCSB).

Passive Verbs

The passive is formed when the receiver of an action becomes the subject of the sentence rather than the original doer, such as in the sentence "A man is justified by faith." (Romans 3:28b, NIV). "Faith" is the doer here, so if the sentence were active, it would read, "Faith justifies a man."

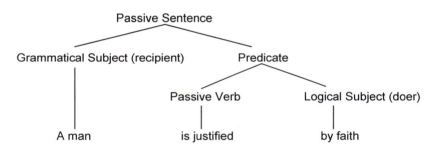

We use the passive to emphasize the recipient of the action rather than the doer.

- *Glorious things* **are said** *of you, O City of God.* (Psalm 87:3, NIV). The emphasis in this verse lies on the glorious things said about the City of God. Whoever is doing the action (saying) is not important. Had the verse said, "Everyone says glorious things of you, O City of God," we automatically focus our attention on who *everyone* is. With the passive verb, we focus on the main idea, the glory of the City of God.

The original doer of the action is sometimes indicated by a "by-phrase" (underlined in the following sentences).

- *For all have sinned and fall short of the glory of God, and* **are justified** <u>by his grace</u> *as a gift, through the redemption that is in Christ Jesus.* (Romans 3:23-24, ESV). The by-phrase lets us know who or what does the action. The Messiah's gift of grace justifies us.
- *Then Jesus* **was led up** <u>by the Spirit</u> *into the wilderness to be tempted by the devil.* (Matthew 4:1, NASB). The passive ("was led up") has a by-phrase to show us the original doer of the action. In this case, the Holy Spirit led Jesus into the wilderness. However, the use of the passive verb puts the emphasis on Jesus rather than on the Holy Spirit.

When the passive is used and there is no by-phrase to show the doer of the action, we need to use the context and make assumptions about the doer of the action or we need to conclude that the doer of the action is not important.

- *For what **can be known** about God is plain to them, because God has shown it to them. For his invisible attributes, namely, his eternal power and divine nature, **have been** clearly **perceived**, ever since the creation of the world, in the things that **have been made**. So they are without excuse.* (Romans 1:19-20, ESV). Here, context shows us, even without a by-phrase, that people are the ones who can know and perceive God's attributes, such that they are without excuse. The context also tells us that we could add "by God" to the phrase "the things that have been made."

- *"Though the mountains **be shaken** and the hills **be removed**, yet my unfailing love for you **will not be shaken** nor my covenant of peace **be removed**,"* says the LORD, who has compassion on you. (Isaiah 54:10, NIV). Here, no doer is indicated for the shaking and removing of the mountains. We would have to conclude that the doer is not important here. The most interesting part, however, comes in the latter half of the verse. The negative passives indicate no doer of the action at all. No one can shake God's love nor remove God's covenant of peace.

The Divine Passive

In the Bible, unless the context suggests another doer of the action, the implication is that the doer is God. We could add the by-phrase of "by God" to these Scriptural sentences. We could call this occurrence "the divine passive."

For example, some claim that God is not in the book of Esther simply because the author never mentions his name. However, consider the following verse with a passive.

- *Who knows if perhaps you **were made** queen for just such a time as this?* (Esther 4:14b, NLT). Although God is not explicitly mentioned, by recognizing the divine passive, we can see that God is working.

Additional examples can be found other places in Scripture.

- *Now when the thousand years have expired, Satan **will be released** from his prison.* (Revelation 20:7a, NKJV). Who will release Satan at the end of the thousand years? God holds the power.

- *But the angel said to him: "Do not be afraid, Zechariah; your prayer **has been heard**."* (Luke 1:13, NIV). Though it does not say who heard his prayer, it is implied that God was listening.

- *While he was blessing them, he left them and **was taken up** into heaven.* (Luke 24:51, NIV). Although the verse does not state explicitly who took Jesus up into heaven, the implication is that God did so.

Salvation, whether immediate physical salvation or eternal salvation of the soul, is expressed with a passive verb, showing that God saves us. We do not save ourselves through our own actions.

- *Restore us, LORD God of Hosts; look on us with favor, and we **will be saved**.* (Psalm 80:19, HCSB).

- *All people will hate you because you follow me, but those people who keep their faith until the end **will be saved**.* (Mark 13:13, NCV).

- *I am the door. If anyone enters by me, he **will be saved** and will go in and out and find pasture.* (John 10:9a, ESV). This verse reveals the origin of salvation, Jesus, who is "the door." Notice the other verbs in contrast to the passive. The verb "enters" is an action taken by "anyone"; it is not a passive done by God. Also, the verbs "will go" and "[will] find" are actions that are completed by the saved Christian.

- *Blessed are those whose lawless deeds* ***have been forgiven***, *and whose sins* ***have been covered***. (Romans 4:7, NASB). Notice that this sentence is inverted (see Chapter 3). The passive verbs show the divine passive. The lawless deeds have been forgiven by God and the sins have been covered by God.

It is interesting to note whenever a passive verb is combined with a progressive or perfect verb. Notice that the following verse has a present progressive passive verb.

- *And in him you too* ***are being built*** *together to become a dwelling in which God lives by his Spirit.* (Ephesians 2:22, NIV). The progressive in this sentence implies that the building is a present, ongoing process, and the passive voice in the verse tells us that we are not doing the building process. Also, there is no by-phrase, and we can see that this verse has a divine passive, the action done by God.

Sometimes a Bible sentence has a mixture of active and passive verbs.

- *For with the heart one* ***believes*** *and* ***is justified***, *and with the mouth one* ***confesses*** *and* ***is saved***. (Romans 10:10, ESV). Notice the two types of verbs used in this sentence. In each clause, the first verbs are active: "believes" and "confesses." Those are actions that we as Christians do. The second verb in each clause is passive because the action is being done by God: "is justified" and "is saved."
- *And it shall come to pass that whoever* ***calls on*** *the name of the LORD* ***shall be saved***. (Acts 2:21, NKJV). "Calls on" is an active verb. That is an action that we can do. The passive verb "shall be saved" reminds us that we do not save ourselves.
- *Our lives are a Christ-like fragrance rising up to God. But this fragrance is perceived differently by those who* ***are being saved*** *and by those who* ***are perishing***. (2 Corinthians 2:15, NLT). The first verb is present progressive passive. The present progressive shows a continuing process. The passive, again, shows that we are being saved; we are not the doer of the action. The second verb ("are perishing") is present progressive, but not passive. That verb states a situation (some people are perishing), but it does not use a passive such as "are being destroyed." So, while salvation is represented as the divine passive, an action done by God, the opposite (perishing) is not expressed in this verse as being caused by God.

Emphatic Verbs

We make verbs emphatic in Edited American English by placing a form of the verb DO in front of the rest of the verb in a statement. Therefore, to be more emphatic in English, we would say, "I **did** do something." We assume that if the translators of Scripture found an emphatic verb in the original language, they used an emphatic verb in English.

- *We* ***do*** *have such a high priest, who sat down at the right hand of the throne of the Majesty in heaven, and who serves in the sanctuary, the true tabernacle set up by the Lord, not by man.* (Hebrews 8:1-2, NIV). The emphatic verb leaves no doubt that we can have confidence and rest in knowing that our high priest exists and oversees all with complete divine authority.
- *Then Judah said, "Let her keep what she has, or we will become a laughingstock. After all, I* ***did*** *send her this young goat, but you didn't find her."* (Genesis 38:23, NIV). In order to justify himself, Judah is emphasizing that he did what was required of him to fulfill his pledge.

Questions for Analyzing Verbs in Bible Sentences

In summary, when trying to understand the significance of verbs in Scripture, ask and answer these questions:

1. Find each verb and look at the tense. Is the verb present, past, or future? What implications does that have for the meaning of the sentence?
2. Look for progressive, perfect, and conditional verbs.
    - If the verb is perfect, consider how the tense affects the timing and meaning of the verb phrase.
    - If the verb is progressive, note that the action has a duration.
    - If the verb is conditional, look for the auxiliary verb that marks it as conditional. What conditions does the auxiliary place on the verb and how does this affect the meaning?
3. Find any imperatives in the passage.
    - Who is making the command? For example, is the command coming from God?
    - To whom is the command being given? Is the instruction meant for us today?
    - What is the context of the imperative? Are there any conditions or further explanations attached to the command or instruction?
4. Find the passive verbs.
    - Remember that a passive will emphasize the original direct object of the sentence. What does the use of a passive verb suggest to the meaning of the passage?
    - Is there a by-phrase in the sentence? If so, who is the doer of the action?
    - If there is no by-phrase, does context suggest a doer of the action?
    - Is the passage an example of the divine passive? If so, what does that imply?
    - Particularly if there is a combination of passive verbs and active verbs, check the passive verbs to see if God is at work and check the other verbs to see what they are expressing about the subject.
5. Look for any emphatic verbs. Why is the action emphasized in this way?

Some Practice

Psalm 100

- *Shout joyfully to the LORD, all the earth. Serve the LORD with gladness; come before Him with joyful singing. Know that the LORD Himself is God; it is He who has made us, and not we ourselves; we are His people and the sheep of His pasture. Enter His gates with thanksgiving and His courts with praise; give thanks to Him, bless His name. For the LORD is good; His lovingkindness is everlasting and His faithfulness to all generations. (NASB).*

This passage has seven imperative sentences in it, which means the psalm is full of commands. Since "all the earth" is commanded to "shout joyfully," we can assume that the commands are being given to us as well. There are several conditions that accompany the command; they are marked in bold below.

- *Shout **joyfully to the LORD**, all the earth. Serve the LORD **with gladness**; come **before Him with joyful singing**. Know that the LORD Himself is God; it is He who has made us, and not we ourselves; we are His people and the sheep of His pasture. Enter His gates **with thanksgiving** and His courts **with praise** give thanks **to Him**, bless His name. For the LORD is good; His lovingkindness is everlasting and His faithfulness to all generations. (NASB).*

In addition to the commands, we have present tense linking verbs. In the sentence "Know that the LORD Himself is God," we find a linking verb and a predicate nominative ("God"). In the last sentence, the three present tense linking verbs are followed by predicate adjectives. The implications of predicate nominatives and predicate adjectives are explained in Chapter 2, but it is worth note here that the present tense is used. God **is**, not **was**. The third sentence, "it is he who has made us, and not we ourselves," is extraposed (see Chapter 3). By wording it in this manner, the psalmist is able to draw attention to God as the Maker. Finally, notice the present perfect tense in "has made." This shows an action that happened in the past but the resulting condition or situation continues in the present. We continue to be his creation.

Ephesians 6:10-19

- *Finally, my brethren, be strong in the Lord and in the power of His might. Put on the whole armor of God, that you may be able to stand against the wiles of the devil. For we do not wrestle against flesh and blood, but against principalities, against powers, against the rulers of the darkness of this age, against spiritual hosts of wickedness in the heavenly places. Therefore take up the whole armor of God, that you may be able to withstand in the evil day, and having done all, to stand. Stand therefore, having girded your waist with truth, having put on the breastplate of righteousness, and having shod your feet with the preparation of the gospel of peace; above all, taking the shield of faith with which you will be able to quench all the fiery darts of the wicked one. And take the helmet of salvation, and the sword of the Spirit, which is the word of God; praying always with all prayer and supplication in the Spirit, being watchful to this end with all perseverance and supplication for all the saints. (NKJV).*

This entire passage is a number of commands strung together. These actions are not mere possibilities, but they become something that Christians must do. Notice that accompanying the commands are phrases explaining both how to do the commands and why.

Matthew 6:33-34

- *But seek first His kingdom and His righteousness, and all these things will be added to you. So do not worry about tomorrow; for tomorrow will care for itself. Each day has enough trouble of its own. (NASB).*

First, this passage starts with an imperative (command). We are commanded to seek God's kingdom and His righteousness. The second verb is a conditional passive. The condition imposed by "will" tells us that it will be in the future. The passive is very interesting because the passage says that all these things (what we need to live) will be added (or given) to us. God provides. The last imperative ("do not worry about tomorrow") is accompanied by an explanation.

Chapter 5
Noun Structures

In Chapter 2, we identified some nominal (noun) structures as they appear in the primary functions of subject, direct object, predicate nominative, and indirect object. In this chapter, we will take a closer look at noun structures. Being able to identify and understand the significance of the noun structures in a sentence is important for grasping the total meaning of the sentence. We will examine some interesting aspects of noun structures and explore implications for interpretation of Scripture.

Pronouns in Scripture

Identifying Pronouns

In English, nouns are often replaced with pronouns. Below are lists of pronouns.

Demonstrative Pronouns this that these those	**Quantifier Pronouns** most all many much few each some any more several every either neither enough no
	Indefinite Pronouns everybody nobody somebody anybody everyone no one someone anyone everything another nothing others something anything
	Reflexive Pronouns myself ourselves itself yourself himself herself themselves yourselves
	Personal Pronouns she her him he I it they we *one me you them us *sometimes a personal pronoun

Significance of Pronouns in Bible Sentences

Noticing pronouns gives added depth to Bible study. First, it is important to know to whom or what the pronoun is specifically referring in order to understand exactly what is being said. This will be discussed in more detail in Chapter 6. In addition, noticing pronouns can add insight that might otherwise be missed. The following verses illustrate this.

- *Then God said, "Let **us** make man in **our** image, after **our** likeness."* (Genesis 1:26a, ESV). In this verse, the pronouns "us" and "our" refer to God. It is interesting to note that God refers to himself with a plural pronoun, suggesting God's Trinitarian nature.
- ***All** have turned away, **they** have together become worthless.* (Romans 3:12a, NIV). The quantifier pronoun "all" provides important information about who needs salvation: all have fallen from God's glory and are therefore "worthless."
- ***Everything** is nonsense.* (Ecclesiastes 1:2a, CEV). When used here, the indefinite pronoun "everything" helps create the broad, generalizing statement that is being made. This pronoun is purposefully vague, and the verses that follow it in Ecclesiastes 1 help explain what is meant by "everything."
- *The kingdom of the world has become the kingdom of our Lord and of His Christ; and **He** will reign forever and ever.* (Revelation 11:15b, NASB). Here is an interesting pronoun usage. The singular "he" seems to refer to both "Lord" and "Christ," making these two into one.
- *And the little **ones** that **you** said would be taken captive, **your** children who do not yet know good from bad—**they** will enter the land. **I** will give **it** to **them** and **they** will take possession of **it**.* (Deuteronomy 1:39, NIV). The pronoun "I" mentioned in this verse is God. "You" and "your" refer to the older generation of Israelites, and "they" and "them" are used in reference to the

children of the Israelites, the younger generation. "It" is the Promised Land. The parents and older members of the group of Israelites feared their children's captivity to the giants living in the land God was going to give them. God held the older generation responsible for doubting Him and for refusing to enter the Promised Land when He told them to do so. Therefore, the older ones are not included in the pronoun "they," which describes those who will take possession of the land.

- *If **any of you** is deficient in wisdom, let **him** ask of the giving God, Who gives to **everyone** liberally and ungrudgingly, without reproaching or faultfinding, and **it** will be given **him**.* (James 1:5, Amplified). The interesting pronoun here is a cluster of words: "any of you." It is significant that the pronoun is inclusive; anyone can ask for wisdom from God.

Determiners with Nouns in Scripture

Identifying Determiners

Determiners are words that are used in front of nouns. They are not used in front of pronouns, and they are not adjectives. In English, we have five classes of determiners that come before nouns.

Articles	Demonstratives	Possessive Pronouns		Determiner Quantifiers (representative list)			
a	this	his	my	most	each	more	several
an	that	her	our	some	few	either	any
the	these	its	their	neither	every	enough	much
	those	your		another	no	many	all
Genitive Determiners							
This stands for genitive (possessive) noun. It can be either a proper noun (*Paul's*) or a common noun (*the tall man's*). Look for a noun with an apostrophe (usually *'s;* sometimes *s'*).							
Pre-Determiners							
Sometimes in English we use a word before the determiner. This is usually a word such as "both" or "all," such as in the following verses.							
• *David and **all** the Israelites were celebrating with **all** their might before God, with songs and with harps, lyres, tambourines, cymbals and trumpets.* (1 Chronicles 13:8, NIV).							
• *For to this end Christ died and rose and lived again, that he might be Lord of **both** the dead and the living.* (Romans 14:9, NKJV).							
• *Then **all** his brothers and **all** his sisters and all who had known him before came to him, and they ate bread with him in his house; and they consoled him and comforted him for **all** the adversities that the LORD had brought on him.* (Job 42:11, NASB).							

Significance of Determiners with Nouns in Bible Sentences

Although determiners may seem trivial and insignificant, they can provide important insight into the noun that follows. Often, they add a personal tone, necessary information, or a clarification about the noun. Watch how determiners (in bold) are being used in the following verses.

- ***The** Lord is **my** shepherd.* (Psalm 23:1a, NKJV). Within this verse, we encounter first the definite article "the." Here, this determiner establishes God as the one and only Lord. This definite but non-personal determiner is followed by a more personal determiner "my." God is not only <u>the</u> Lord; he is also <u>my</u> shepherd, the personal, intimate one who loves me.
- *"**My** God, **my** God, why have you abandoned me?"* (Mark 15:34b, NLT). When Christ says this while he is hanging on the cross, he uses the personal "my," suggesting intimacy and close

relationship. Noticing the "my" adds even more emotional depth to the separation that was taking place between Father and Son.

- *All Scripture is God-breathed and is useful for teaching, rebuking, correcting and training in righteousness, so that the man of God may be thoroughly equipped for every good work.* (2 Timothy 3:16, NIV). The quantifier determiner that is used here ("all") makes it clear that not only parts of Scripture are inspired, but that "all" is God-breathed.

- *This Book of the Law shall not depart from your mouth…* (Joshua 1:8a, NASB). The demonstrative determiner "this" plays the important role of pointing something out and letting us know that the noun is specific, not general. "This" refers to the one and only book of the law that was given to Moses. Using the demonstrative determiner here makes sure that the noun is only one very definite thing. The article "the" is definite; it is not a law but the law. The determiner "your" refers to the hearers (or readers).

- *"I am the Lord's servant."* (Luke 1:38a, NIV). First, we have the article "the." We are talking about "the" Lord, not "a" lord. Second, we have an example of a genitive determiner. Notice the apostrophe showing ownership ("Lord's"). When used, the genitive reveals possession and belonging. Here, when Mary says this to the angel, it displays her submission to God's sovereignty and her status of belonging to him.

- *We proclaim him, admonishing and teaching everyone with all wisdom, so that we may present everyone perfect in Christ. To this end I labor, struggling with all his energy, which so powerfully works in me.* (Colossians 1:28-29, NIV). In the second sentence, the determiner "this" in front of "end" refers to Paul's desire to "present everyone perfect in Christ." Paul labors and struggles with the energy God has provided to present everyone perfect in Christ by proclaiming him and admonishing and teaching everyone with all wisdom.

- *You have set your glory above the heavens.* (Psalm 8:1b, ESV). The possessive determiner "your" signifies ownership. In this case, it is God who owns his glory and has glorified himself above all else. It is interesting to note that God's glory is something that is described as owned by God and thus controlled by God.

- *I will also make you a light for the Gentiles, that you may bring my salvation to the ends of the earth.* (Isaiah 49:6b, NIV). God refers to his salvation with the possessive determiner "my." Using the possessive determiner ensures that we understand that salvation belongs to God; it is from him and through him. It is not just "a salvation," "salvation," or even "the salvation," but God's salvation.

- *In addition to all, taking up the shield of faith with which you will be able to extinguish all the flaming arrows of the evil one.* (Ephesians 6:16, NASB). Note the pre-determiner in this verse ("all"). Faith is not victorious over only some of Satan's temptations; it can conquer all of them. The pre-determiner emphasizes the inclusiveness. The definite article "the" is also used three times here. There is a specific shield of faith (not a shield) and "the" evil one (not merely an evil one).

- *We do have such a high priest, who sat down at the right hand of the throne of the Majesty in heaven, and who serves in the sanctuary, the true tabernacle set up by the Lord, not by man.* (Hebrews 8:1b-2, NIV). The pre-determiner here ("such") makes the meaning quite different than it would be without it. With the "such," the meaning is "that kind of."

Predicate Nominatives in Scripture

Identifying Predicate Nominatives

A predicate nominative is a noun structure that follows a linking verb (usually *is, am, was, are, were, will be,* or some other form of the verb *BE*). We looked at predicate nominatives briefly in Chapter 2.

- *Together you are the body of Christ.* (1 Corinthians 12:27a, CEV).

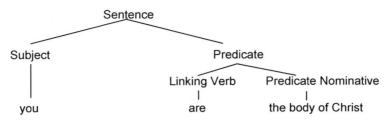

Significance of Predicate Nominatives in Bible Sentences

A predicate nominative renames or helps define the subject. However, in English a single predicate nominative does not claim to be a full definition of the subject. For example, when we say, "He is a minister," we are not saying that being a minister is the entire essence of that man; it does not fully rename or define him. Part of the definition would also be that he is a son, a graduate, a friend, and so forth. The same principle applies to biblical sentences with predicate nominatives. They might merely contribute to the definition of the subject, so <u>we should not automatically assume that a predicate nominative is furnishing a full definition of the subject</u>.

Notice in the following example that while God's love for honesty and integrity is portrayed, the predicate nominative (in bold) does not provide a full definition of the subject (underlined).

- *A false balance* is **an abomination to the LORD**, but *a just weight* is **his delight**. (Proverbs 11:1, ESV). "A just weight," a weight that does not rob or cheat or distort, is "his delight," but "his delight" is not a full definition of a just weight nor is a just weight a full definition of "his delight." Similarly, "an abomination to the Lord" is not a full definition of "a false balance."

When the predicate nominative is a list, we can more likely assume that the list comprises a complete definition of the subject.

- But *the fruit of the Spirit* is **love, joy, peace, patience, kindness, goodness, faith, gentleness, self-control**. (Galatians 5:22-23a, HCSB). When the Spirit is at work within a Christian's life, his work is seen through the presence of the qualities listed above. It is interesting to observe that the verb is singular rather than plural, even though the list is multiple objects, indicating that the fruit exits as a whole rather than in pieces; we are meant to have it in its entirety.

Sometimes the predicate nominative is literal. However, <u>in the Bible, often the subject and predicate nominative form a metaphor</u>. A metaphor makes a comparison of two otherwise unlike items, saying that one is not literally the other but that they share a common characteristic. In the following examples of metaphors, the subject is underlined and the predicate nominative is in bold.

- *For <u>we</u> are to God **the aroma of Christ among those who are being saved and those who are perishing**.* (2 Corinthians 2:15, NIV). Here, Christians ("we") are said to be "the aroma of Christ." Just as an aroma grabs people's attention and draws them nearer, wanting to breathe more of it in, Christians should be drawing people to Christ and making Christ more desirable through how we live our lives.
- *Together <u>you</u> are the **body of Christ**, and <u>each one of you</u> is **a part of that body**.* (1 Corinthians 12:27, NCV). Paul here uses the metaphor of the unity of a body to help us understand what relationships between Christians should look like. In a body, every part is essential for proper functioning. Christians, who have different gifts and abilities, need each other in order to form a properly functioning church. Each Christian is "a part of the body."
- *If I speak in the tongues of men and of angels, but have not love, <u>I</u> am only **a resounding gong or a clanging cymbal**.* (1 Corinthians 13:1, NIV). The metaphor in this verse compares the speaker, who speaks "in the tongues of men and of angels" to a gong or cymbal. Without love,

our skills and abilities may be big, loud, and attention getting, but they will not be meaningful or be used to their full capacity, bringing glory to God.

- *They* are **the shoot I have planted, the work of my hands, for the display of my splendor**. (Isaiah 60:21, NIV). In this verse, Isaiah is referring to the Israelites. God had planted them in the Promised Land, he had created them, and he made them to bring him glory and to display his splendor.

Noun Appositives in Scripture

Identifying Noun Appositives

A final type of nominal structure (a structure that functions as a noun) that has important implications for the meaning of a biblical sentence is called an appositive. Appositives follow a noun or noun cluster and rename it or partially define it. They are similar in function to predicate nominatives, but they appear directly after the noun cluster (in Edited American English) rather than after a BE verb. The noun cluster that an appositive renames is called the head. Since they are attached to any noun cluster, appositives may be found anywhere in a sentence. Appositives are generally set off with commas but may also follow a colon. In the following example, the head is underlined and the appositive is in bold.

- *If I am delayed, you will know how people ought to conduct themselves in God's household, which is* <u>the church of the living God</u>, **the pillar and foundation of the truth**. (1 Timothy 3:15, NIV). "The pillar and foundation of the truth" renames "the church of the living God."

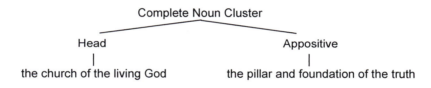

As is true with the head to which they are attached, appositives can take various forms (a noun cluster, gerund phrase, infinitive phrase, or a noun clause). Do not let the terms (such as *gerund phrase*, *infinitive phrase*, or *noun clause*) cause you to become confused. It is not important for Bible study that you can distinguish among these grammatical structures since they all function as nominals or noun structures. <u>What we are trying to do here is to find the head and the appositive that follows it. Then we can examine the meaning that the renaming or defining of the appositive is adding to the head</u>. In the examples below, the head is underlined and the appositive is in bold.

Sometimes an appositive is a simple noun or noun cluster.

- *For he has rescued us from the domain of darkness, and transferred us to the kingdom of his beloved Son, in whom we have* <u>redemption</u>, **the forgiveness of sins**. (Colossians 1:13-14, NASB). In this verse, we can see how important the appositive ("the forgiveness of sins") is because it defines redemption.

Sometimes an appositive is a gerund phrase. A gerund phrase begins with an *-ing* form of a verb, and the entire phrase is used as a noun in a sentence.

- *And we pray this in order that you may live a life worthy of the Lord and may please Him in* <u>every way</u>: **bearing fruit in every good work, growing in the knowledge of God, being strengthened with all power according to His glorious might so that you may have great endurance and patience, and joyfully giving thanks to the Father, who has qualified you to share in the inheritance of the saints in the kingdom of light**. (Colossians 1:10-12, NIV).

Notice that the compound gerund appositive is a list of "-ing phrases" that define what the author means by "every way."

Sometimes an appositive is an infinitive phrase. An infinitive phrase in English usually begins with the word *to* followed by a verb.

- *For I have <u>the desire</u> **to do what is good**, but I cannot carry it out.* (Romans 7:18, NIV). The infinitive phrase "to do what is good" renames "the desire." It identifies the particular desire.

Finally, sometimes an appositive is an entire noun clause, including its subordinator word followed by its own subject and predicate.

- *For I am confident of <u>this very thing</u>, **that He who began a good work in you will perfect it until the day of Christ Jesus.*** (Philippians 1:6, NASB). The noun clause appositive ("*that he who began a good work in you will perfect it until the day of Christ Jesus*") renames and defines the head "this very thing." It identifies the thing of which Paul is confident.

There might even be more than one appositive.

- *But you are <u>a chosen generation</u>, **a royal priesthood, a holy nation, His own special people**, that you may proclaim the praises of Him who called you out of darkness into His marvelous light.* (1 Peter 2:9, NKJV). Notice that each appositive helps define the chosen generation.

Always identify the head along with the appositive, and be sure to find the complete head and complete appositive.

- *I pray also that the eyes of your heart may be enlightened in order that you may know <u>the hope to which he has called you</u>, **the riches of his glorious inheritance in the saints**.* (Ephesians 1:18, NIV). The appositive "the riches of his glorious inheritance in the saints" identifies "the hope to which he has called you." It is important to have the complete head ("the hope to which he has called you") because that helps us identify the hope. It is also important to have the complete appositive ("the riches of his glorious inheritance in the saints") because the complete appositive explains the riches.
- *For they themselves report concerning us the kind of reception we had among you, and how you turned to God from idols to serve the living and true God, and to wait for <u>his Son from heaven, whom he raised from the dead</u>, **Jesus who delivers us from the wrath to come**.* (1 Thessalonians 1:9-10, ESV). In this verse, "Jesus, who delivers us from the wrath to come" renames "his Son from heaven, whom he raised from the dead." Notice that both the head and the appositive in this verse give us important information.

Significance of Noun Appositives in Bible Sentences

Appositives are significant because they give us, within the context of the passage, a definition of the noun they are renaming. They clarify and specify what the noun-cluster head is. They often add a new dimension to the sentence, adding deeper insight. In the following examples, the head is underlined, and the appositive is in bold.

- *From <u>Paul</u>, **a servant of God, and an apostle of Jesus Christ**.* (Titus 1:1a, NCV). Paul often starts his letters by putting an appositive after his name to describe himself as a writer to a group of Christian readers. The appositive establishes his credentials.
- *And you He made alive, who were dead in trespasses and sins, in which you once walked according to the course of this world, according to <u>the prince of the power of the air</u>, **the spirit who now works in the sons of disobedience**.* (Ephesians 2:1-2, NKJV). Notice that in the appositive, "the spirit who now works in the sons of disobedience," we learn more about the

head, "the prince of the power of the air." The appositive gives us important information about Satan: that he is now working in those who are disobedient.

- *Simon Peter answered, "You are* <u>*the Christ*</u>*,* **the Son of the living God**.*"* (Matthew 16:16, NIV). In this sentence, "the Christ" is the head and "the Son of the living God" is the appositive. Notice how we could place an equal sign between the head and the appositive like this: "the Christ" = "the Son of the living God." The appositive gives us a new definition of who Christ is, emphasizing his divinity and relationship to the Father.

- *If* <u>*I*</u> *then,* **your Lord and Teacher***, have washed your feet, you also ought to wash one another's feet.* (John 13:14, ESV). Jesus, speaking to his disciples after washing their feet, defines himself as the disciples' "Lord and Teacher." The appositive, defining Jesus as "Lord and Teacher," makes Christ's servant-like act of washing the disciples' feet even more significant.

- *Though now you do not see Him, yet believing, you rejoice with joy inexpressible and full of glory, receiving* <u>*the end of your faith*</u>—**the salvation of your souls***.* (1 Peter 1:8b-9, NKJV). "The salvation of your souls" redefines or clarifies the head, which is "the end of your faith." Notice how much more is added to the sentence with the appositive. The goal of our faith, the culmination and final work, is the salvation of our souls.

- *Then Mary took about* <u>*a pint of pure nard*</u>*,* **an expensive perfume***.* (John 12:3a, NIV). The appositive and head in this verse are interesting. Mary's act of anointing Christ becomes even more special when we know that "a pint of pure nard" is "an expensive perfume." The appositive works to clarify the head and add meaning.

- *Yet I considered it necessary to send to you* <u>*Epaphroditus*</u>*,* **my brother, fellow worker, and fellow soldier, but your messenger and the one who ministered to my need***.* (Philippians 2:25, NKJV). In this verse, the appositive does a good job of defining Epaphroditus for us. Not only is the appositive a tribute to that man, but it also teaches us about the roles we take as Christians: brothers, fellow workers, and fellow soldiers. Finally, the long appositive in this sentence helps us as modern-day readers to understand the context of this passage: who has been involved and what he has done.

- *Watch out for* <u>*those dogs*</u>*,* **those people who do evil, those mutilators who say you must be circumcised to be saved***.* (Philippians 3:2, NLT). There are two appositives for the head "dogs": "those people who do evil" and "those mutilators who say you must be circumcised to be saved." These certainly clarify for us whom Paul meant by "dogs."

- *But for that very reason I was shown mercy so that in* <u>*me*</u>*,* **the worst of sinners***, Christ Jesus might display his unlimited patience as an example for those who would believe on him and receive eternal life.* (1 Timothy 1:16, NIV). Paul defines himself in the appositive as "the worst of sinners." He is aware that, in and of himself, he is unworthy of God's love. He acknowledges his past of persecuting Christians and recognizes Christ's mercy and patience in his life.

- *Here is the main point: We have a High Priest who sat down in the place of honor beside the throne of the majestic God in heaven. There he ministers in* <u>*the heavenly Tabernacle*</u>*,* **the true place of worship that was built by the Lord and not by human hands***.* (Hebrews 8:1-2, NLT). In this passage, the appositive, "the true place of worship that was built by the Lord and not by human hands," is referring to a sanctuary that exists in heaven. The sanctuary in which the priests of Bible times served was "a copy and shadow of what is in heaven." (Hebrews 8:5).

- *And when eight days had passed, before His circumcision, His name was then called* <u>*Jesus*</u>*,* **the name given by the angel before He was conceived in the womb***.* (Luke 2:21, NASB). Luke 1:26-38 is the record of the angel Gabriel telling Mary that she would have a son whom she was to name Jesus. The appositive in Luke 2:21 not only explains who had decreed Jesus' name ("the angel"), but it also tells when the name was given: "before he had been conceived."

- *He said to them, "Take <u>nothing for your trip</u>, **neither a walking stick, bag, bread, money, or extra clothes**."* (Luke 9:3, NCV). Before sending his disciples out, Jesus provides packing guidelines in this verse. The list in the appositive defines what he means by "nothing for your trip."
- *Look now, you are depending on <u>Egypt</u>, **that splintered reed of a staff, which pierces a man's hand and wounds him if he leans on it**! Such is Pharaoh king of Egypt to all who depend on him.* (Isaiah 36:6, NIV). In this verse, the king of Assyria sends a message defining Egypt as a splintered staff. The appositive definitely gives us insight into his opinion of Egypt.
- *The LORD has broken <u>the staff of the wicked</u>, **the scepter of rulers, that struck the peoples in wrath with unceasing blows, that ruled the nations in anger with unrelenting persecution**.* (Isaiah 14:5-6, ESV). This head has an extensive appositive following it. Besides defining for us what "the staff of the wicked" is, notice that the description in the long appositive gives us a good idea of what these wicked rulers have been doing.

Sometimes the translators of the Scriptures have moved the appositive to the end of the sentence for stylistic reasons.

- *<u>Such a high priest</u> meets our need—**one who is holy, blameless, pure, set apart from sinners, exalted above the heavens**.* (Hebrews 7:26, NIV). The appositive used to describe the high priest is much longer in this verse than the actual main thought: "Such a high priest meets our need." By placing the appositive at the end, the translators place more emphasis on the qualities of this high priest.

Intensifiers

Intensifiers are a type of appositive, and like other appositives, they follow a noun cluster or pronoun. However, rather than simply redefining a noun, they draw attention to it or <u>intensify</u> it. Intensifiers are just one word long, a reflexive pronoun. The reflexive pronouns are *myself, ourselves, himself, herself, itself, themselves, yourself,* and *yourselves.* Watch for a noun or pronoun directly followed by a reflexive pronoun to signal an intensifier. In the following Bible sentences, the head is underlined and the intensifier is in bold.

- *"Do not be afraid, O worm Jacob, O little Israel, for <u>I</u> **myself** will help you," declares the LORD, your Redeemer, the Holy One of Israel.* (Isaiah 41:14, NIV). The Lord is speaking to the Israelites here, and the adjectives ("worm" and "little") contrast with his power. It is significant, then, that the intensifier tells them that God will personally help them.
- *The <u>Spirit</u> **Himself** testifies with our spirit that we are children of God.* (Romans 8:16, NASB). In this sentence, extra attention is given to "the Spirit" by having the intensifier "himself" following it. The intensifier makes it significant that it is God's Spirit that testifies with our spirit that we belong to Him.
- *Not only that, but we also who have the firstfruits of the Spirit, even <u>we</u> **ourselves** groan within ourselves, eagerly waiting for the adoption, the redemption of our body.* (Romans 8:23, NKJV). The intensifier in this sentence not only adds emphasis to "we" but also adds contrast. Paul has just finished saying how all of creation groans as it awaits redemption. Now he turns and says that the Christians, the redeemed, also groan. "Ourselves" helps to create the juxtaposition as well as the emphasis on "we." The second use of the word "ourselves" is not acting as an intensifier but merely a reflexive pronoun.
- *Therefore, since <u>I</u> **myself** have carefully investigated everything from the beginning, it seemed good also to me to write an orderly account for you, most excellent Theophilus, so that you may know the certainty of the things you have been taught.* (Luke 1:3-4, NIV). Here, the intensifier after "I" gives Luke's account even more authority. The emphasis is that Luke did the research

himself for the things he wrote, thus making them reliable. Using "myself" emphasizes Luke's careful work.

- *He **himself** bore our sins in his body on the tree, that we might die to sin and live to righteousness.* (1 Peter 2:24a, ESV). The intensifier "himself" adds emphasis to "he." This addition is crucial in this sentence because it highlights that Christ personally bore our sins.

Questions for Analyzing Noun Structures

In summary, when trying to understand the significance of noun structures in Scripture, ask and answer these questions:

1. Find any pronouns in the passage. What significance or meaning does the use of that particular pronoun add?

2. Find any determiners that come before the nouns. What tone, necessary information, or clarification about the noun do the determiners add?

3. Find any predicate nominatives. Is the predicate nominative literal or a metaphor?

- If the predicate nominative is literal, does it provide a complete definition of the subject or is it a partial identification?

- If the predicate nominative is figurative (a metaphor), what does it add to the understanding of the subject?

4. Find any appositives and the heads that they follow. Make sure that you have identified the complete head and the complete appositive.

- How does the appositive clarify and specify what the noun-cluster head is?

- How does the appositive add a new dimension to the sentence, adding deeper insight?

5. Find any intensifiers in the passage. What important information does the use of the intensifier add?

Some Practice

James 1:27

- *Religion that God our Father accepts as pure and faultless is this: to look after orphans and widows in their distress and to keep oneself from being polluted by the world.* (NIV).

Here, a demonstrative pronoun ("this") serves as a predicate nominative that is literal rather than metaphorical. The head is "this"; after the colon, the appositive (a compound infinitive phrase) renames the head to tell us what "this" is. The appositive tells us what God expects of us if we align ourselves with him. The instructions in the appositive are emphasized. Serving as somewhat of a teaser, the demonstrative pronoun adds to the emphasis. The verse could be written more concisely, but the extra words make us spend more time on the sentence and its meaning.

Philippians 1:21

- *For to me to live is Christ, and to die is gain.* (ESV).

The first noun to pay attention to is the personal pronoun "me." Paul is talking about himself, using himself as an example. Why? Paul was a respected apostle of Jesus Christ. He was adding credence to the words by reminding us that this is his life's work, passion, and philosophy—not something he heard from someone else. Following the personal pronoun are two sentences with two predicate nominatives. They mirror each other to highlight the contrast they present ("live" and "die"); each subject is an infinitive phrase ("to live" and "to die") acting as a noun. Paul is being quite literal here, communicating that each of the opposite options that he has result in good things.

1 Corinthians 1:18

- *For the message of the cross is foolishness to those who are perishing, but to us who are being saved it is the power of God.* (NIV).

The determiner "the" is important in this verse because it communicates uniqueness. This is not just "a" message about "a" cross; it is *the* message of *the* cross. The same is true of *the* power of God. The pronouns "those" and "us" are used to specify two different groups of people. The demonstrative pronoun "those" is defined by the clause "who are perishing," and the personal pronoun "us" is defined by "who are being saved."

Ephesians 1:13-14

- *In Him you also trusted, after you heard the word of truth, the gospel of your salvation; in whom also, having believed, you were sealed with the Holy Spirit of promise, who is the guarantee of our inheritance until the redemption of the purchased possession, to the praise of His glory.* (NKJV).

In this passage, there is an appositive "the gospel of your salvation" attached to its head, "the word of truth," providing further clarification and definition. Here, the determiners are very crucial; "*your* salvation" is a personal salvation that is for you as an individual. In the same way, "*our* inheritance," and "*his* glory" both hold significant implications as to the ownership of these qualities. There is also a linking verb inside what is called a relative clause (see chapter 7), "who **is** the guarantee of our inheritance until the redemption of the purchased possession." The subject here is implied to be "the Holy Spirit of promise," and the predicate nominative is everything after the verb until the comma; the Holy Spirit is the guarantee of our inheritance. This is a good example of a predicate nominative that does not fully rename or define its head. It is true that the Holy Spirit is the guarantee of our inheritance, but much more must be included if we were to provide a complete definition. Therefore, this appositive does not fully rename and redefine the Holy Spirit.

John 1:14

- *The Word became flesh and took up residence among us. We observed His glory, the glory as the One and Only Son from the Father, full of grace and truth.* (HCSB).

First, notice all the pronouns and the importance of these small words. The Word took up residence "among us," directly in our midst as Jesus, fully man and fully God. Also, the word "one" can be both a pronoun and a number; here it is a pronoun referring to Jesus. Also, in the second sentence, "the glory as the one and only Son from the Father, full of grace and truth," is an appositive renaming "his glory." Another interesting aspect of this sentence is the use of a definite determiner. Each of the nouns "Word," "glory," "One," and "Father" are preceded by "the," showing that they are all specific and known, not general or abstract.

Proverbs 10:20a

- *The tongue of the righteous is **choice silver**.* (NKJV).

Here is a predicate nominative that creates a metaphor. The tongue is obviously not literally made of silver. A metaphor compares two unlike objects (in this case a tongue and choice silver) by saying that the two objects have one characteristic in common. In this case, the characteristic is that they are valuable. The value of the words of the righteous is highlighted by saying that "the tongue of the righteous" (by which truthful, kind words are produced) is "choice silver," a precious metal.

Chapter 6
Connecting Elements

This chapter covers grammatical elements that refer to other parts of the text or connect parts of the text. We need to look beyond the specific sentence to the context of the passage. Correct understanding of the Bible often depends upon an understanding of these elements.

Significance of Pro-forms in Bible Sentences

The term "pro-form" refers to a word or group of words that refers to another word or group of words. As such, pro-forms have a **referent**, something to which they refer. The most common pro-form is the class of pronouns.

Pronouns

Personal pronouns and **demonstrative pronouns** have an antecedent or referent. As we saw in Chapter 5, possessive pronouns are a type of determiner; they also have an antecedent. That is, they refer to something else. In this sense, these pronouns are connecting elements. In Scripture sentences, it is always important to find the antecedent of the pronoun.

> **Personal Pronouns:** *she he it they I we her him them me us you*

We need to make sure that we connect the antecedent to the pronoun before we can understand the verse. To find the antecedent, we usually need to look at the verse or verses that come before. In the following passages, the pronouns are in bold.

- *They are brought to **their** knees and fall, but **we** rise up and stand firm.* (Psalm 20:8, NIV). It is important to know to whom "they," "their," and "we" are referring for an accurate understanding of the verse. When we look at Psalm 20:7, we see that "they" and "their" refer to people who "trust in chariots and horses" and "we" refers to those who "trust in the name of the Lord" (Psalm 20:7). This verse contrasts the results of trusting in God with the results experienced by those who put their faith in their own resources.

- *He predestined **us** to adoption as sons through Jesus Christ to **Himself**, according to the kind intention of **His** will, to the praise of the glory of **His** grace, which **He** freely bestowed on **us** in the Beloved. In **Him** **we** have redemption through **His** blood, the forgiveness of **our** trespasses, according to the riches of **His** grace which **He** lavished on **us**.* (Ephesians 1:5–8a, NASB). In the second half of the passage, the bolded pronouns "him," "his," and "he" do not all share the same antecedent. The antecedent of "him" seems to be "the Beloved," referring to Jesus Christ (v. 6). The first "his" also has Jesus Christ as its antecedent, as Jesus shed His blood for our forgiveness. The second "his" seems to refer to "the God and Father of our Lord Jesus Christ" (v. 3). The final "he" also has God as its antecedent. It is especially important in this particular passage to examine context. Any of these masculine pronouns could refer to either the Father or Jesus the Son, but context helps determine their exact reference. The pronouns "our" and "us" refer to Christians. Paul uses them in this section of Scripture in reference to himself and Ephesian believers.

- *Your eyes saw **my** unformed body. All the days ordained for **me** were written in **your** book before **one** of **them** came to be. How precious to **me** are **your** thoughts, O God! How vast is the sum of **them**! Were **I** to count **them**, **they** would outnumber the grains of sand. When **I** awake, **I** am still with **you**.* (Psalm 139:16-18, NIV). The pronouns "you" and "your" are used in reference to God ("O God," v.17). "My," "me," and "I" refer to David, the writer of this psalm.

There are several uses of the pronoun "them." The antecedent of the first appearance of this word is "all the days ordained for me." The pronoun "one" also refers to "all the days ordained for me." The second and third uses of "them" refer to God's thoughts, as does the pronoun "they." In this passage, it is important to clarify the antecedent of each of the many pronouns.

- *And **I** said to **you**, "**You** have come to the hill country of the Amorites, which the LORD **our** God is giving **us**."* (Deuteronomy 1:20, ESV). The pronoun "I" refers to Moses, God's chosen leader for his people. "Our" and "us" include both Moses and the entire nation of Israel, and "you" refers to the people of Israel. It is important here to understand the context to identify the antecedent; earlier in the chapter "Moses spoke to the people of Israel according to all that the LORD had given him in commandment to them." (Deuteronomy 1:3 ESV). The antecedent is also used for the purpose of emphasis. In this verse, Moses refers to the Lord "our" God, but in verse 21, he refers to the Lord "your" God, with a different emphasis, perhaps to strengthen the faith of the people.

> **Demonstrative Pronouns**: *this   that   these   those*

The **demonstrative pronouns** can be very important to the understanding of Scripture. We need to make sure that we always know the referent for these as well, especially since the referent might be in preceding verses.

- *But we belong to God, and those who know God listen to us. If they do not belong to God, they do not listen to us. **That** is how we know if someone has the Spirit of truth or the spirit of deception.* (1 John 4:6, NLT). The demonstrative pronoun "that" is worth noticing. Demonstrative pronouns point things out in a noticeable way, drawing our attention to something we might otherwise miss. Here, "that" refers to the earlier part of the verse, talking about the listening qualities of people. One can recognize the Spirit of truth in a person who listens to the apostles and Christians.

- *By **this** we know love, that he laid down his life for us, and we ought to lay down our lives for the brothers.* (1 John 3:16, ESV). This is an example of the writer's using the demonstrative pronoun first ("this") and then explaining what "this" is. Again, notice how the demonstrative pronoun "this" draws our attention to the important statement about what love is. Our understanding is incomplete without going on to understand how we know what love is.

- *Wonderful are Your works, and **that** my inner self knows right well.* (Psalm 139:14b, Amplified). This psalm was written by David (the pronoun "I" is in reference to him) and is a declaration of praise to God (the pronoun "your" refers to God). What did David know well? The pronoun "that" refers to the inverted clause "wonderful are your works" (see Chapter 3).

- ***All this** took place to fulfill what the Lord had said through the prophet.* (Matthew 1:22, NIV). In this sentence, the subject is very vague, "all this." In order to understand the sentence, it is necessary to look at the entire context and figure out what "all this" is. In this case, it is referring to Christ's birth through Mary. We can understand this by reading the entire chapter which talks about the birth of Christ, and also by the next verse, which records what the Lord said through the prophet: "The virgin will be with child and will give birth to a son, and they will call him Immanuel"—which means, "God with us." (Matthew 1:23, NIV). The entire context shows that Christ's birth fulfilled "what the Lord had said."

- *Convinced of **this**, I know that I will remain and continue with you all for your progress and joy in the faith.* (Philippians 1:25, NASB). Of what is it that Paul is convinced? We need to look for the link to the verses before this in which he says, "But I am hard-pressed from both directions, having the desire to depart and be with Christ, for that is very much better; yet to remain on in the flesh is more necessary for your sake." (Philippians 1:23-23, NASB). Paul is convinced that he will remain in this life because the Philippians need him.

Sometimes even **indefinite pronouns** will need to be defined. The indefinite pronouns are listed below.

> **Indefinite Pronouns:** *everybody   anybody   somebody   nobody   anything   everything   nothing*
> *something   everyone   anyone   someone   no one   another   others*

It might seem as if the words "everyone" and "anyone" are fairly straightforward, but we still need to look to the context.

- *My dear brothers, take note of this: **Everyone** should be quick to listen, slow to speak and slow to become angry.* (James 1:19, NIV). Who is "everyone"? The beginning of the sentence tells us that it does not mean everyone in the world; instead, the "everyone" here is the "dear brothers," or fellow followers of Christ.

Other Pro-forms

Pro-forms are structures in a sentence that substitute for other words, phrases, or clauses. Pro-forms usually consist of the word "*so*" or the phrases "*do so*" or "*did so.*"

- *And in fact, you do love all the brothers throughout Macedonia. Yet we encourage you, brothers, to **do so** more and more* (1 Thessalonians 4:10, NIV). In this verse, the word "do" appears twice, but only one appearance is actually a pro-form. The first "do" from "you do love" forms an emphatic verb, putting emphasis on the action of loving (see Chapter 4). The second occurrence, "do so," is a pro-form, substituting for "love all the brothers throughout Macedonia." Paul wants them to love all the brothers more and more.
- *And not only **so**, but we glory in tribulations also: knowing that tribulation worketh patience.* (Romans 5:3, KJV). The pro-form "so" refers to Paul's last statement: "and rejoice in hope of the glory of God" (Romans 5:2b). Paul is saying that we do not only rejoice in "hope of the glory of God," but we also glory "in tribulations."
- *Some, to be sure, preach Christ out of envy and strife, but others out of good will. These **do so** out of love, knowing that I am appointed for the defense of the gospel.* (Philippians 1:15-16, HCSB). First, notice the ellipsis in the first sentence: "others [preach Christ] out of good will" (see Chapter 3). In the second sentence, "these" refers to the "others" mentioned in the first sentence (those who preach out of good will). The pro-form "do so" refers to action taken by the "others": they preach the Gospel of Christ.
- *And not only **so**, but ourselves also, who have the first-fruits of the Spirit, even we ourselves groan within ourselves, waiting for our adoption, to wit, the redemption of our body* (Romans 8:23, ASV). In this verse, "so" refers to the subject of Romans 8:22, which is the groaning of creation: "For we know that the whole creation groaneth and travaileth in pain together until now." (Romans 8:22, ASV). Paul says that in addition to the groaning of creation for God's kingdom to come, we Christians are groaning and longing for our adoption and the redemption of our bodies.

Significance of Conjunctions in Bible Sentences

Conjunctions are words that link parts of a sentence (or multiple sentences) together. They are joining words that show the relationship between words or thoughts.

Coordinating Conjunctions

Coordinating conjunctions are the simplest type of conjunctions, and an easy way to remember these conjunctions is by the acronym FANBOYS, formed by the first letter of each word.

Coordinating Conjunctions: *for   and   nor   but   or   yet   so*

Coordinating conjunctions may link parts of sentences (words or phrases). They may also link two grammatical sentences to form compound sentences. Finally, while your grade school teacher probably told you never to start a sentence with *and* or *but,* this happens regularly in Scripture (and in most non-academic and informal writing). In these cases, the sentence starting with a coordinating conjunction is being linked to the sentence that precedes it. These conjunctions convey a similar meaning, whether they appear in the middle of a sentence or at the beginning.

Coordinating conjunctions are used to link two parts of a sentence that are very directly related to each other. The conjunction between the two is an important signal telling *how* the two thoughts are related.

AND   The word *and* signals that the two thoughts are linked, related, and considered equal. In a narrative, the "and" often means "and then," showing a sequence of events.

- *Give thanks to Him **and** bless His name.* (Psalm 100:4b, NLT). The use of "and" shows that thanking God and blessing His name are two related activities.
- *Who may stand in His holy place? He who has clean hands **and** a pure heart, who does not lift up his soul to an idol or swear by what is false.* (Psalm 24:3b-4, NIV). In order to stand before God, one must be clean on the outside and the inside. "Clean hands" and a "pure heart" are requirements together.
- *If I live, it will be for Christ, **and** if I die, I will gain even more.* (Philippians 1:21, CEV). Paul speaks of his win-win situation in this verse. Paul's contentment with his current state of living for Christ was equal to the contentment and peace he felt about his eventual death, in which he would gain by being united with Christ.
- ***And** whatever you do or say, do it as a representative of the Lord Jesus, giving thanks through him to God the Father.* (Colossians 3:17, NLT). In this example, "and" is very significant because verse 17 is the final statement in this section of Colossians 3, which concerns rules for holy living. This verse contains an overarching principle that applies to verses 1-16. Obedience to God involves living our lives in Jesus' name and for God's glory.
- *Other seeds fell among thorns, **and** the thorns grew up and choked them.* (Matthew 13:7, ESV). Here the "and" means "and then."

BUT/YET   The words *but* and *yet* are important words in the study of Scripture; they signal a contrast.

- *I shall not die, **but** live, and declare the works of the Lord.* (Psalm 118:17, KJV). The use of "but" contrasts the sharp distinction between death and life.
- ***But** God demonstrates His own love for us in this: While we were still sinners, Christ died for us.* (Romans 5:8, NIV). Contrasting with the previous verse, this verse shows how God's love is different from the love of humans. Romans 5:7 discusses how "very rarely anyone will die for a righteous man." A human who is willing to die for a good, righteous person is hard to find, but God let his perfect Son die for unrighteous sinners.
- *Hope deferred makes the heart sick, **but** desire fulfilled is a tree of life.* (Proverbs 13:12, NASB). There is a sharp contrast shown between a life of an unfulfilled hope and one that is fulfilled.
- *A gentle answer turns away wrath, **but** a harsh word stirs up anger.* (Proverbs 15:1, NIV). Not only does a gentle answer bring about positive results, but also the opposite, a harsh word, brings about negative results.

- *Other seeds fell on rocky ground, where they did not have much soil, and immediately they sprang up, since they had no depth of soil,* **but** *when the sun rose they were scorched. And since they had no root, they withered away.* (Matthew 13:5-6, ESV). This conjunction indicates a contrast between the first part of the passage (in which the reader may believe that everything is well) and the second part (that shows that it is not good to sow among rocks, even if the immediate outcome looks positive).

OR/NOR   The coordinating conjunction *or* can signal a choice, an alternative. It also might be signaling that the two thoughts are not simultaneous; they are at odds with each other. We use *nor*, the negative form of *or*, when the part of the sentence that precedes the *nor* has a negative element of some sort.

- *I am the LORD; that is my name; my glory I give to no other,* **nor** *my praise to carved idols.* (Isaiah 42:8, ESV). Here, the use of "nor" adds to the list of things that the Lord will <u>not</u> give away. He will not give away his glory or his praise.
- *The rest of mankind that were not killed by these plagues still did not repent of the work of their hands; they did not stop worshiping demons, and idols of gold, silver, bronze, stone and wood— idols that cannot see or hear or walk.* **Nor** *did they repent of their murders, their magic arts, their sexual immorality, or their thefts.* (Revelation 9:20-21, NIV). The first verse has two negative statements: they did not repent, and they did not stop worshipping demons and idols. The "nor" before the continued list of their sins emphasizes their lack of repentance. In Edited American English, we would not use "nor" to start a new sentence; these two would be one sentence.
- *And Lebanon is not sufficient to burn,* **nor** *its beasts sufficient for a burnt offering.* (Isaiah 40:16, NKJV). Lebanon is shown to be lacking in two ways in this verse. Not only are its forests insufficient for altar fires, but it also lacks sufficient animals to sacrifice.

FOR   When used in this sense, *for* generally means "because" and indicates that a reason for the previous statement is coming.

- *Oh, give thanks to the Lord* **for** *He is good!* (Psalm 136:1, NKJV). The use of "for" gives a reason for thanking the Lord: He is good.
- *Therefore if you have been raised up with Christ, keep seeking the things above, where Christ is, seated at the right hand of God. Set your mind on the things above, not on the things that are on earth.* **For** *you have died and your life is hidden with Christ in God.* (Colossians 3:1-3, NASB). This verse provides the reason why Christians no longer need to focus on earth, because we have been "raised up with Christ" and so we should now focus on "where Christ is."
- *Fear not,* **for** *I have redeemed you.* (Isaiah 43:1b, NIV). God not only tells his people not to fear, but he also provides a reason for not fearing.
- *Take counsel together, but it will come to nothing; speak a word, but it will not stand,* **for** *God is with us.* (Isaiah 8:10, ESV). Isaiah writes with complete confidence in God. The reason that the plan and strategy of the nations would be thwarted and would not stand was God's presence and support.

SO   The conjunction *so* lets the reader know that the following thought is a consequence or an effect caused by whatever was mentioned previously.

- *Again the Israelites did what was evil in the Lord's sight,* **so** *the Lord handed them over to the Philistines, who oppressed them for forty years.* (Judges 13:1, NLT). Because the Israelites sinned and did evil, the Lord responded to their disobedience by handing them over to the Philistines. This shows a cause and effect relationship. Their forty years under the Philistines was not arbitrary; rather, it was a direct result of their decision to sin.

Subordinating Conjunctions

Subordinating conjunctions join structurally unequal phrases to illustrate their differences. Sentences with subordinating conjunctions always have an independent (main) clause and a subordinate clause, which begins with a subordinating conjunction. The subordinate clause can come before or after the independent clause.

Words that Can Function as Subordinating Conjunctions											
after	*although*	*as*	*because*	*before*	*for*	*if*	*lest*	*once*	*provided*	*since*	
though	*when*	*till*	*unless*	*until*	*whenever*	*where*	*wherever*	*whether*	*while*		

Words that Can Function as Cluster Subordinating Conjunctions			
as if	*as long as*	*as soon as*	*as though*
even though	*in order that*	*no matter how*	*even if*
in as much as	*so that*	*in so far as*	*whether or not*

Like coordinating conjunctions, subordinating conjunctions show the relationship between the two clauses that they join. Subordinating conjunctions show perhaps an even stronger relationship because one clause is always subordinate to (dependent on) the other. An understanding of this relationship is critical to the understanding of the sentence. The examples below show some of the relationships that can exist.

- *Although He was a Son, He learned obedience from the things which He suffered.* (Hebrews 5:8, NASB). The use of the subordinating conjunction "although" shows that the action is not necessarily customary or expected. It would be expected that a Son would learn obedience directly from his Father rather than from the things that he suffered. It could also be unexpected that God's Son would need to learn obedience at all.

- *A son honors his father, and a servant his master. **If** then I am a father, where is my honor? And **if** I am a master, where is my fear? says the LORD of hosts to you, O priests, who despise my name.* (Malachi 1:6, ESV). God states a known cultural custom: fathers and masters are to be honored. He then shows the connection with the subordinating conjunction. The "if" signals an existing situation. If God is a father (which he is) and a master (which he is), then his people should be showing him the appropriate honor.

- *The people stood far off, **while** Moses drew near to the thick darkness where God was.* (Exodus 20:21, ESV). The "while" conjunction shows that the two actions happened at the same time.

- *These kings will go to war against the Lamb. But he will defeat them, **because** he is Lord over all lords and King over all kings.* (Revelation 17:14, CEV). The clause "he is Lord over all lords and King over all kings" provides the reason why the Lamb will be victorious.

- *"Bring the whole tithe into the storehouse, **so that** there may be food in My house, and test Me now in this," says the Lord of hosts, "if I will not open for you the windows of heaven and pour out for you a blessing **until** it overflows.* (Malachi 3:10, NASB). The clause following the conjunction "so that" tells us what the result of tithing will be, and the conjunction "until" tells us to what extent we will be blessed.

- *As for the man who does this, whoever he may be, may the LORD cut him off from the tents of Jacob—**even though** he brings offerings to the LORD Almighty.* (Malachi 2:12, NIV). "Even though" is a subordinating conjunction that relates the dependent clause to the independent clause because it anticipates an objection that may have arisen. It helps the reader know how seriously the Lord considers his commands.

- **Whenever** *I would restore the fortunes of my people,* **whenever** *I would heal Israel, the sins of Ephraim are exposed and the crimes of Samaria revealed.* (Hosea 6:11b-7:1, NIV). This subordinating conjunction further explains what will happen in the future, giving us details of events that will happen under certain conditions. At the same time that God's people are restored and Israel is healed, the sins and crimes of Ephraim and Samaria will also be exposed.

Often coordinating and subordinating conjunctions are used in the same verse.

- *My dear children, I am writing this to you* **so that** *you will not sin.* **But** *if anyone does sin, we have an advocate who pleads our case before the Father. He is Jesus Christ, the one who is truly righteous.* (1 John 2:1, NLT). John states that his purpose ("so that") is to keep these people from sinning. The "but" signals a contrast in that if they do sin, there is still hope.
- *If we claim we have not sinned, we are calling God a liar* **and** *showing that his word has no place in our hearts.* (1 John 1:10, NLT). The subordinating conjunction "if" makes a cause and effect connection between the first and second parts of the verse. The "and" signals that there is a compound effect. If we say we have not sinned, then we call God a liar as well as demonstrate a lack of respect for his word.
- *You priests should be eager to spread knowledge,* **and** *everyone should come to you for instruction,* **because** *you speak for me, the LORD All-Powerful.* (Malachi 2:7, CEV). The coordinating conjunction "and" shows that the two actions are related, and the subordinator "because" introduces the clause that explains the reason that these two actions should happen.

Adverbial Conjunctions

Adverbial conjunctions can be either words or phrases that join one sentence to the previous sentence, showing relationships like addition, contrast, result, space, or time. They are set apart from the rest of the sentence, usually by a comma, and can be found at any number of places in the sentence.

Some Words that Can Function as Adverbial Conjunctions					
therefore	*likewise*	*also*	*rather*	*still*	*hence*
nonetheless	*otherwise*	*furthermore*	*finally*	*similarly*	*first*
however	*accordingly*	*moreover*	*too*	*eventually*	*next*
then	*notwithstanding*	*nevertheless*	*last*	*besides*	

The following passages demonstrate how adverbial conjunctions add important meaning to the sentences.

- *It took Solomon thirteen years,* **however,** *to complete the construction of his palace.* (1 Kings 7:1, NIV). The adverbial conjunction "however" signals a contrast. The verse before this one tells us that it took seven years to complete the temple. The adverbial conjunction highlights the fact that he spent more time on his own house than he did on the house of God.
- *Put to death* **therefore** *what is earthly in you: sexual immorality, impurity, passion, evil desire, and covetousness, which is idolatry.* (Colossians 3:5, ESV). The adverbial conjunction "therefore" signals a result or reason for a previous statement. This verse tells us to put sin to death, but the "therefore" suggests that the previous verse gives a reason for doing so. The previous verse states: "When Christ who is your life appears, then you also will appear with him in glory." (Colossians 3:4, ESV). God has saved us and will bring us to glory; therefore, we should put to death things that do not honor him. Also notice the noun appositive ("sexual

immorality, impurity, passion, evil desire, and covetousness, which is idolatry") explaining the head ("what is earthly in you") (see Chapter 5).

- ***First of all,*** *the Jews were entrusted with the whole revelation of God.* (Romans 3:2b, NLT). This adverbial conjunction tells us that this is the beginning of some sort of series.
- ***Finally,*** *brothers, whatever is true, whatever is honorable, whatever is just, whatever is pure, whatever is lovely, whatever is commendable, if there is any excellence, if there is anything worthy of praise, think about these things.* (Philippians 4:8, ESV). The use of "finally" suggests a connection to the rest of the passage. Paul is telling the church at Philippi to rejoice and to not worry, but rather present requests to God. The fact that this verse includes the "finally" implies that this is the last in the series of commands regarding fear and worry.
- *"**Also,** from today on I am He alone, and no one can take anything from My hand. I act, and who can reverse it?"* (Isaiah 43:13b, HCSB). This verse comes at the end of a passage about the identity of God, so the "also" serves to reinforce all the statements about God that came before and to build on them.
- ***Instead,*** *it should consist of the hidden person of the heart with the imperishable quality of a gentle and quiet spirit, which is very valuable in God's eyes.* (1 Peter 3:4, HCSB). The "instead" signals a contrast that Peter is drawing here between a surface level of beauty as determined by the world and the deeper beauty valued by God.

The choice of the conjunction can slightly affect the meaning or emphasis of the material. An examination of various versions might show this.

- ***Moreover, as*** *you Philippians know…* (Philippians 4:15, NIV).
- *You yourselves **also** know, Philippians…* (Philippians 4:15, NASB).
- ***And*** *you Philippians yourselves know…* (Philippians 4:15, ESV).
- ***Now*** *you Philippians know **also**…* (Philippians 4:15, NKJV).
- ***As*** *you know, you Philippians…* (Philippians 4:15, NLT).
- ***And*** *you, Philippians, know…* (Philippians 4:15, HCSB).

It is obvious that the overall meaning of the verse (even the phrase) is not dramatically altered, but each version gives its own emphasis. The ESV and the HCSB, with their use of a simple coordinating conjunction, may not cause the reader to look back for context as readily as the NIV, with its use of the word "moreover." The "also" in the NASB and NKJV is next to the verb and so tells us specifically that the Philippians know other things as well as what Paul is about to tell them. The NLT indicates that they know what follows, but it is the only version that does not connect the ideas to the preceding ones.

Significance of Whole-Sentence Modifiers in Bible Sentences

Certain other structures in English also give some context or connections in Bible sentences. These phrases modify the sentence as a whole.

Absolutes

Absolutes are unique structures that modify the entire sentence. They are formed by taking a phrase with a "BE" verb ("their consciences **are** bearing witness") and dropping the "BE" verb ("their consciences bearing witness") and placing that phrase in another complete sentence.

Absolutes are not very common, but they often give important context or information for what is found in the rest of the sentence.

- *Indeed, when Gentiles, who do not have the law, do by nature things required by the law, they are a law for themselves, even though they do not have the law, since they show that the requirements of the law are written on their hearts, **their consciences also bearing witness,*** *and their thoughts now accusing, now even defending them.* (Romans 2:14-15, NIV). There are two absolutes; they give us insight into what is happening inside the Gentiles' minds. Even though they do not know the requirements of the law, they have the ability to make ethical decisions.

Nouns of Direct Address

Vocatives, or nouns of direct address, are simply people or things that are being directly spoken to in a sentence. Often understanding who is being addressed is critical to a complete understanding of a sentence or passage.

- **My dear children**, *I'm writing this to you so that you will not sin. But if anybody does sin, we have one who speaks to the Father in our defense—Jesus Christ, the Righteous One.* (1 John 2:1, NIV). The apostle John is writing as an elderly man to believers all over the world. He is explaining his motive as being loving, not judgmental. This term of endearment shows us his authority as a respected man of God, as well as his love for the church.
- *I love thee,* **O Jehovah, my strength**. (Psalm 18:1, ASV). Names are meaningful psychological tools. When we hear our name spoken, we listen more closely. There is no mistaking that the words are for us. By using God's name, the psalmist gives unashamed adoration to the Lord.
- *Hear,* **O heavens**! *Listen,* **O earth**! *For the Lord has spoken: "I reared children and brought them up, but they have rebelled against me."* (Isaiah 1:2, NIV). This is ironic. God is speaking to the heavens and the earth as the ones who will listen whereas the people whom he created have rebelled.
- *He rebuked Peter and said, "Get behind me,* **Satan**; *for you are not setting your mind on God's interests, but man's."* (Mark 8:33b, NASB). Christ is talking to Peter and yet addresses Satan. In doing so, Jesus emphasizes the sinful nature of Peter's act in the previous verse.
- *Finally,* **brothers**, *whatever is true, whatever is honorable, whatever is just, whatever is pure, whatever is lovely, whatever is commendable, if there is any excellence, if there is anything worthy of praise, think about these things.* (Philippians 4:8, ESV). Paul addresses those he writes to as brothers, showing equal status and a loving relationship. Also, since they are "brothers," they are Christians.
- *So then,* **my dear friends**, *just as you have always obeyed, not only in my presence, but now even more in my absence, work out your own salvation with fear and trembling.* (Philippians 2:12, HCSB). The vocative "my dear friends" sets an affectionate tone for the recipients of Paul's instructions.
- **Timothy**, *guard what has been entrusted to your care.* (1 Timothy 6:20, NIV). Timothy is receiving instructions about how to be a good church leader. He was entrusted with the specific guardianship of the church in Ephesus.

Often "you" is a noun of direct address. However, we must make sure that we note the entire vocative so that we understand exactly who "you" is in the sentence.

- **You who preach that a man should not steal**, *do you steal?* (Romans 2:21, NKJV). Here Paul is talking to Jews who trust in the Law and are teaching others.
- *I write to* **you, fathers**, *because you have known Him who is from the beginning. I write to* **you, young men**, *because you have overcome the evil one. I write to* **you, dear children**, *because you have known the Father.* (1 John 2:13, NIV). John covers all stages of life and all levels of spiritual maturity. He wants the readers to know that his message applies to everyone.
- *But as for* **you, O man of God**, *flee these things. Pursue righteousness, godliness, faith, love, steadfastness, gentleness.* (1 Timothy 6:11, ESV). Paul is addressing Timothy specifically in this passage, but his teaching can be extended to include all Christians.

- *Hear, **you deaf**! And look, **you blind**, that you may see.* (Isaiah 42:18, NASB). For a literally blind or deaf person, these commands would be frustrating. God is talking to those who have shut their eyes and covered their ears to who he is and what he has done.
- *Awake, **you drunkards**, and weep, and wail, **all you drinkers of wine**, because of the sweet wine, for it is cut off from your mouth.* (Joel 1:5, ESV). Joel is revealing a word from God (Joel 1:1, ESV) and speaking to Israel, so in this case, "you" is referring to those in Israel who are doing these things. God is convicting them of not only their sin, but also the way their sin has kept them from acting against the evil in the land.
- ***Zion, herald of good news**, go up on a high mountain. **Jerusalem, herald of good news**, raise your voice loudly.* (Isaiah 40:9, HCSB). The entire vocative is necessary in order to understand why the voice should be raised loudly: they are heralds of good news.

Other Sentence Introducers

We sometimes use modifiers for a whole sentence that do not connect to any other sentences as do adverbial conjunctions. Some modern examples are *obviously, invariably, perhaps, frankly, undoubtedly, unfortunately, luckily, to our amazement,* and *to tell the truth.* These words and expressions often set the tone for the sentence. For example, in the Bible, words and phrases such as "indeed," "truly," and "I tell you the truth" emphasize the truths that follow them.

- ***Indeed**, before the day was, I am He.* (Isaiah 43:13, NKJV). Here the use of "indeed" emphasizes the unquestionable truth of God even "before the day was."
- ***Indeed**, you were concerned before, but you lacked opportunity.* (Philippians 4:10b, NASB). Paul shows that he understands and believes that those in Philippi were concerned even though they were only recently able to act on their concern for him.
- ***You see**, at just the right time, when we were still powerless, Christ died for the ungodly.* (Romans 5:6, NIV). The whole-sentence modifier sets an instructive tone.
- ***Truly**, you are a God who hides himself, O God of Israel, the Savior.* (Isaiah 45:15, ESV). Isaiah is explaining God's present actions compared to the deliverance that he would later bring through Cyrus of Persia.
- ***I tell you the truth**, the man who does not enter the sheep pen by the gate, but climbs in by some other way, is a thief and a robber.* (John 10:1, NIV). This introducer commands us to believe what is said. Jesus is talking, and what he says is true.

Questions for Analyzing Connecting Elements

In summary, when trying to understand the significance of connecting elements in Scripture, ask and answer these questions:

1. Find any personal pronouns and possessive pronouns.
   - What is the antecedent? (To find the antecedent, we need to look to the material that precedes the pronoun.)
   - How does knowing the antecedent help you understand the verse?
2. Find any demonstrative pronouns. Look usually at the verses that precede it. To what does the demonstrative pronoun refer?
3. Find any indefinite pronouns. Look at the context to make sure that the meaning of the indefinite pronoun is clear.
4. Find any pro-forms (usually consist of the word "*so*" or the phrase "*do so*"). What concepts are these words substituting for?
5. Find the coordinating conjunctions. What does the specific conjunction that is being used add to the meaning?

- ***And*** signals that the two thoughts are related, linked, and equal. In a narrative, "and" might mean "and then."
- ***But*** or ***yet*** signals a contrast.
- ***Or*** gives a choice or an alternative or also might be signaling that the two thoughts are not simultaneous or are at odds with each other. ***Nor*** is used when the sentence has a negative element.
- ***For*** generally means "because" and indicates that a reason for the previous statement is coming.
- ***So*** lets the reader know that the following thought will be a consequence or an effect caused by whatever was mentioned previously.

6. Find any subordinating conjunctions. What relationship are they signaling?

7. Find any adverbial conjunctions, usually starting the verse. They show a relationship with the material that precedes it. What relationship is being shown?

8. Find any whole-sentence modifiers.
- If there is an absolute, what important information or context does it provide?
- If there is a noun of direct address, who, exactly, is being addressed in that verse? What is the significance of knowing who is being addressed?
- If there is a sentence introducer, what tone does it set for what follows?

Some Practice

John 17:7-9

- *Now they know that everything you have given me comes from you. For I gave them the words you gave me and they accepted them. They knew with certainty that I came from you, and they believed that you sent me. I pray for them. I am not praying for the world, but for those you have given me, for they are yours.* (NIV).

This passage illustrates pronouns and antecedents as well as coordinating conjunctions. To understand the passage, we have to understand the context so that the antecedents are clear. Knowing that Jesus is praying to God clarifies the first person and second person pronouns. The antecedent to the "they" and "them" is the disciples, as indicated by the previous verse: "those whom you gave me out of this world." (John 17:6, NIV). The use of "and" shows a connection, that the two beliefs of the disciples about the origin of Christ are linked and equal, emphasizing their certain belief in Christ's connection to God. The use of "but" in the next verse signals a contrast between the world in general and those people in the world whom God gave to Christ, namely the disciples.

1 Corinthians 16:5-6

- *I plan to go through Macedonia, so I will come to you after I go through there. Perhaps I will stay with you for a time or even all winter. Then you can help me on my trip, wherever I go.* (NCV).

To begin with, we need to identify that the personal pronoun "I" refers to Paul, and the personal pronoun "you" refers to the Corinthians. The first sentence includes the coordinating conjunction "so," which signals that coming to them will be the effect of his going through Macedonia, as well as the subordinating conjunction "after," which gives us a sense of the time frame. The "perhaps" is a sentence introducer, showing that Paul is not sure of the length of time. An "or" separates the different options. The adverbial conjunction "then" starting the third sentence is another reference to time.

Ecclesiastes 8:15-17

- *So I commended pleasure, for there is nothing good for a man under the sun except to eat and to drink and to be merry, and this will stand by him in his toils throughout the days of his life which God has given him under the sun. When I gave my heart to knowing wisdom and to see the task which has been done on the earth (even though one should never sleep day or night), and I saw every work of God, I concluded that man cannot discover the work which has been done under the sun. Even though man should seek laboriously, he will not discover; and though the wise man should say, "I know," he cannot discover. (NASB).*

The passage begins with the conjunction "so," indicating that what follows is an effect or result caused by whatever was mentioned previously. In the verses that precede this passage, Solomon has been saying that everyone experiences good times and rewards as well as bad times and undeserved miseries. Solomon is frustrated at the injustice in the world. Earlier in the chapter, he says that this is meaningless. Based upon these previous observations and this conclusion ("so"), he recommended the enjoyment of life.

The next word is the first-person pronoun "I." This is significant because Solomon is not speaking for God. He is giving his own thoughts. The personal pronoun "him" refers to "a man under the sun" as does the possessive pronoun "his." Thus, Solomon is not talking about only himself and his own experiences but about all humanity on the earth. The demonstrative pronoun "this" stands for "to eat and to drink and to be merry."

The coordinating conjunction "for" signals that the reason that he commended pleasure will follow ("for there is nothing good for a man under the sun except to eat and to drink and to be merry"). The conjunction "for" usually means "because." The coordinating conjunction "and" in the first sentence shows a related thought linked to the first one.

The subordinating conjunction "when" beginning the second sentence is important here because it shows a different context. While the first sentence is based upon his observation of injustice (signaled by the "so"), the next sentence tells us that now he is trying to know wisdom and to see every work of God. The second conclusion in the passage is based upon this new context, signaled by "when."

Another context is shown by the subordinating conjunction "even though." In both uses, this conjunction is adding the condition of continuous work ("even though one should never sleep day or night" and "even though man should seek laboriously"). The conjunction "though" also adds a condition of the wise man claiming understanding. If Solomon, being the wisest man in the world, was at a loss, no other man on earth stood a chance. Understanding this takes humility and trust. We know that God has it under control even if we can't understand the work of God.

The NIV version of this passage has an absolute.

- *When I applied my mind to know wisdom and to observe man's labor on earth—**his eyes not seeing sleep day or night**—then I saw all that God has done.*

Absolutes give important context or information for the sentence in which they are found. This absolute gives further information about man's labor on earth, a man who works extremely hard, not sleeping.

Chapter 7
Adjectival Structures

The Bible has a number of structures that operate as adjectives. There are two general functions for adjectival structures, but in both cases, they describe a noun structure.

- **Predicate Adjectives** come after a verb and describe the subject.
- **Modifiers** are attached to a noun or pronoun and add descriptive detail. There are many types of modifiers, but they all add descriptive detail.

Identifying Predicate Adjectives

Predicate adjectives follow linking verbs (usually *am, is, was, were, are* or other forms of the verb *BE*). They describe the subject of the clause in which they are found. However, <u>a predicate adjective does not claim to be a full description of the subject.</u> We use predicate adjectives all of the time in English without claiming that we have a full description. When we say, "She is intelligent," we are not saying that intelligence is her only characteristic. The same principle applies to biblical sentences with predicate adjectives. They add descriptive detail to the subject, but we should not automatically assume that a predicate adjective is furnishing a full description of the subject.

In the examples that follow, the subject is underlined, and the predicate adjectives are in bold.

Simple Predicate Adjectives

- <u>*We*</u> *are* **confident***, yes, well pleased rather to be absent from the body and to be present with the Lord.* (2 Corinthians 5:8, NKJV). Here "confident" is the predicate adjective and describes "we." The context of this sentence tells us that "we" refers to Christians. Therefore, the predicate adjective gives us one attribute of Christians.

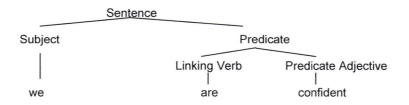

- *Because of the LORD's faithful love, we do not perish, for His mercies never end.* <u>*They*</u> *are* **new** *every morning;* **great** *is* <u>*Your faithfulness*</u>! (Lamentations 3:22-23, HCSB). Here the first predicate adjective is "new" with "they" ("his mercies") as the subject. In the next example, the clause is inverted. That is, the subject and predicate adjective are reversed from their normal order (see Chapter 3). This poetic inversion does not change the meaning of the clause. "Your faithfulness" is the subject and "great" is the predicate adjective.

Notice that in all three cases, the predicate adjective gives descriptive detail about the subject and therefore we learn more about the subject. Remember, however, that the predicate adjective does not necessarily give a full description of the subject. In an example above, the Lord's mercies are "new every morning"; however, additional descriptive words could be used for a full description of these mercies.

When a writer wants a more complete description, he might use more than one predicate adjective.

- But <u>the wisdom from above</u> is first **pure**, then **peaceable, gentle, open to reason, full of mercy and good fruits, impartial** and **sincere**. (James 3:17, ESV). The subject of this sentence ("the wisdom from above") has seven predicate adjectives. This gives us a better description of the "wisdom from above."

Expanded Predicate Adjectives

Another possibility is that the single-word predicate adjective has a structure attached to it, which completes the predicate adjective, adding important detail. The "attachment" to the adjective (called an adjectival complement because it completes the adjective) is necessary to the meaning of the adjective. The entire cluster of words, including the single-word adjective and its attachment, makes up the predicate adjective. It is important that we recognize the entire predicate adjective when we analyze the meaning of a Bible sentence.

For example, in the Bible sentence below, the attachments to the adjective add to the meaning of the predicate adjective. The tree is not merely good; it is "good for food," (a specific meaning to good). The tree is not merely desirable; it is "desirable to make one wise" (specifically giving the type of desirability in this case).

- *When the woman saw that <u>the tree</u> was **good for food**, and that it was a delight to the eyes, and that <u>the tree</u> was **desirable to make one wise**, she took from its fruit and ate; and she gave also to her husband with her, and he ate. (Genesis 3:6, NASB).*

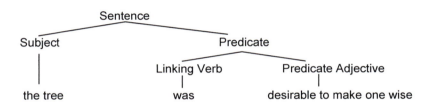

Sometimes a prepositional phrase completes the adjective.

- *Their mouths are **full of cursing and bitterness**. (Romans 3:14, NLT).* Notice that if the prepositional phrase "of cursing and bitterness" were not there, we would be missing important detail about the full mouths.
- *See that no one renders evil for evil to anyone, but always pursue what is **good both for yourselves and for all**. (I Thessalonians 5:15, NKJV).*

Sometimes an infinitive phrase completes the adjective. An infinitive phrase consists of the word *to* followed by a verb phrase and sometimes preceded by a "*for* phrase." In the Bible sentences below, the subjects are underlined, and the adjectives and the infinitive phrases completing those adjectives are in bold.

- *Know this, my beloved brothers: Let <u>every person</u> be **quick to hear, slow to speak** and **slow to anger**. (James 1:19, ESV).* Notice that there are three predicate adjective phrases here to describe the subject "every person." Also notice how the infinitive phrase completes the idea of each adjective and adds important information. One should not be merely quick, but quick to hear; not merely slow, but slow to speak and to anger.
- *But <u>the tax collector</u>, standing some distance away, was even **unwilling to lift up his eyes to heaven**, but was beating his breast, saying, 'God, be merciful to me, the sinner!' (Luke 18:13, NASB).* The tax collector was not merely unwilling, but specifically unwilling "to lift up his eyes to heaven." The entire adjectival cluster is the predicate adjective.

Sometimes other structures complete the adjective.

- *For as <u>the heavens</u> are **higher than the earth**, so are <u>my ways</u> **higher than your ways**, and <u>my thoughts</u> **than your thoughts**.* (Isaiah 55:9, KJV). This verse actually has three predicate adjectives in three clauses.
    - *The heavens are higher than the earth*
    - *My ways [are] higher than your ways*
    - *My thoughts [are higher] than your thoughts*

In the second clause, the normal order has been rearranged a bit (see Chapter 3), and in the third clause, some of the material (in brackets above) is suggested rather than stated (to review ellipsis, see Chapter 3). Nonetheless, we can see that there are three clauses, each with a subject and expanded predicate adjective.

Being able to identify what types of structures are included in these expanded predicate adjectives is not the main point. Rather, we must be sure to include the complete adjective in our consideration of the meaning. The added-on structure completes the meaning of the adjective and therefore adds to what the writer is saying about the subject.

The following predicate adjective ("confident") has an extensive "completer." Paul is not merely "confident"; he is "confident in the Lord that you will take no other view." Consider how the meaning would change if one stopped after the word "Lord." We need the entire predicate adjective to understand how Paul is describing himself here.

- *<u>I</u> am **confident in the Lord that you will take no other view**.* (Galatians 5:10a, NIV).

Similes

The predicate adjective might also be a prepositional phrase. Prepositional phrases acting as predicate adjectives often begin with *like*. This forms a type of comparison that we call a **simile**. A simile compares two otherwise dissimilar things.

- *<u>The kingdom of heaven</u> is **like a man who sowed good seed in his field**.* (Matthew 13:24b, NIV).

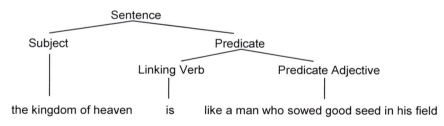

- *<u>The kingdom of heaven</u> is **like treasure hidden in a field**.... Also, <u>the kingdom of heaven</u> is **like a man looking for fine pearls**.* (Matthew 13:44-45, NCV). In these sentences, a prepositional phrase is used to describe the subject, which is "the kingdom of heaven." The prepositional phrases create a comparison by using "like" as the preposition and providing an object of the preposition to which we can compare the "kingdom of heaven." These verses, with prepositional phrases as predicate adjectives, cause us to compare the kingdom of heaven to a man who sowed good seed, to a treasure hidden in a field, and to a man looking for fine pearls. Note that the simile does not say that the kingdom of heaven is actually any of these three things; however, the kingdom of heaven has attributes also evidenced by these three.
- *<u>Starting a quarrel</u> is **like opening a floodgate**.* (Proverbs 17:14a, NLT). Here is another simile, a comparison predicate adjective. This predicate adjective gives a good description of what starting a quarrel is like.

Other Types of Predicate Adjectives

Finally, a predicate adjective might take other forms than the ones we have already seen. In the example below, the predicate adjective is a prepositional phrase, but it is not a simile.

- *What then? Are we better than they? Not at all; for we have already charged that <u>both Jews and Greeks</u> are all **under sin**.* (Romans 3:9, NASB). The predicate adjective in this verse, "under sin," strongly describes the subject ("both Jews and Greeks").

Notice that the following verse has three clauses with predicate adjectives. The first two are single words ("deceitful" and "vain"). The last predicate adjective is actually an infinitive phrase ("to be praised"). We could substitute the word "praiseworthy" for the infinitive phrase "to be praised."

- *<u>Charm</u> is **deceitful**, and <u>beauty</u> is **vain**; but <u>a woman who fears the Lord</u> is **to be praised**.* (Proverbs 31:30, ESV).

Identifying Adjectival Modifiers

The second general function for adjectives is to act as a modifier of a noun structure, describing the noun structure. As we have seen in previous chapters, the noun structure being modified is called a **head**. The adjectival modifier generally comes either directly in front of the head or directly after it. In all of the examples that follow, the head is underlined and the modifier is in bold.

Simple and Expanded Adjectives

Sometimes the adjective is a single word that comes directly in front of a noun. Notice in the following examples that the adjectives describe the noun and add to the meaning of that noun. The adjectives are in bold and the nouns are underlined.

- *As **obedient** <u>children</u>, do not be conformed to the desires of your **former** <u>ignorance</u>.* (1 Peter 1:14, HCSB).
- *There were hangings of **fine white** and **violet** <u>linen</u> held by cords of **fine purple** <u>linen</u> on **silver** <u>rings</u> and **marble** <u>columns</u>.* (Esther 1:6, NASB).
- *His **mighty** <u>arm</u> has done **tremendous** <u>things</u>!* (Luke 1:51a, NLT).
- *The war horse is a **false** <u>hope</u> for salvation; and by its **great** <u>might</u> it cannot rescue.* (Psalm 33:17, ESV).

Notice in the following passage that the single-word adjectives in bold highlight the meaning of the passage by providing contrast.

- *But one who looks intently at the **perfect** <u>law</u>, the law of liberty, and abides by it, not having become a **forgetful** <u>hearer</u> but an **effectual** <u>doer</u>, this man will be blessed in what he does.* (James 1:25, NASB).

Sometimes there is a list of adjectives or even a pair of adjectives joined by a coordinating conjunction such as "and" or "or."

- *Go out to the flocks, and bring me **two fine, young** <u>goats</u>.* (Genesis 27:9a, NLT).
- *He held **seven** <u>stars</u> in his **right** <u>hand</u>, and a **sharp double-edged** <u>sword</u> came out of his mouth.* (Revelation 1:16a, NCV).
- *I have seen a **wicked, violent** <u>man</u> well-rooted like a **flourishing native** <u>tree</u>.* (Psalm 37:35, HCSB).
- ***Blue, purple,** and **red** <u>wool</u>; **fine** <u>linen</u>; **goat** <u>hair</u>* (Exodus 25:4, CEV).

The adjective can also have a qualifier in front of it, such as the word *very* or in the second example, *freshly.*

- *From a **very distant** <u>country</u> your servants have come.* (Joshua 9:9a, ESV).
- *A **freshly plucked** <u>olive leaf</u> was in her mouth.* (Genesis 8:11a, NKJV).

Adjectival Appositives

Sometimes adjectives come right after the noun head. If they come after the noun, they are called adjectival appositives.

- *And Jesus said to him, "Why do you call Me good? No one is good except <u>God</u> **alone**.* (Luke 18:19, NASB). This is an example of a single-word adjective that comes after the noun. "Alone" describes God in the sense that Jesus is saying that only God is good, and therefore, if Jesus is good, he is God.

As we saw with predicate adjectives, biblical adjectival appositives have frequently been expanded with a phrase or even an entire clause. These expanded adjectives that come after the noun head are adjectival appositives.

- *For let not that man suppose that he will receive anything from the Lord; he is <u>a double-minded man</u>, **unstable in all his ways**.* (James 1:7-8, NKJV). The head here is "a double-minded man." Notice that the head has an adjective ("double-minded") in front of the noun to describe the man. "Unstable" is an adjectival appositive, coming after the head, describing the double-minded man of this passage. However, the adjective "unstable" has an adjectival complement that completes the idea of the adjective. The man is not merely unstable; he is "unstable in all his ways." The complement helps clarify the meaning of the adjective: a double-minded man is never sure in his tasks and endeavors.

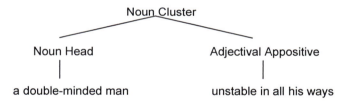

Noun Cluster

Noun Head   Adjectival Appositive

a double-minded man   unstable in all his ways

- *The LORD God said, "It is not good for the man to be alone. I will make <u>a helper</u> **suitable for him**."* (Genesis 2:18, NIV). As we saw with the expanded predicate adjectives, notice that the expansion adds to the meaning. The helper is not merely suitable; she is "suitable for him"; the expansion explains the type of suitability. Considering the context, we see that the adjectival appositive adds meaning. In the Creation narrative in Genesis, Adam has all of the animals, but only the helper that God mentions here will be suitable for Adam.

Prepositional Phrases

In English, we frequently use prepositional phrases for an adjectival function. These prepositional phrases come directly after the noun and add important descriptive detail.

- *You are <u>the salt</u> **of the earth**....You are <u>the light</u> **of the world**.* (Matthew 5:13-14, NKJV). The prepositional phrases in these verses are part of the noun clusters of "salt" and "light." The meaning here is that someone is not merely "salt" or just "light," without a context. "Salt of the earth" and "light of the world" are meaningful ways to describe someone.

Noun Cluster

Noun Head   Adjectival Attachment: Prepositional Phrase

the light   of the world

- In the same way, *you should be* <u>*a light*</u> **for other people***. Live so that they will see the good things you do and will praise* <u>*your Father*</u> **in heaven***.* (Matthew 5:16, NCV). While this prepositional phrase is not absolutely necessary for understanding "Father" (especially in the context of the Sermon on the Mount), it acts with "Father" as a unit of meaning. One important aspect of grouping this phrase within the noun cluster containing "Father" is that it prevents the interpretation of it as an adverbial phrase describing *where* men praise the Father. It seems that the correct understanding of this verse is that the Father is in heaven, not that men are in heaven when they praise the Father.

- *But the goal of our instruction is* <u>*love*</u> **from a pure heart and a good conscience and a sincere faith.** (1 Timothy 1:5, NASB**).** Notice that the long prepositional phrase ("from a pure heart and a good conscience and a sincere faith") describes love and adds to our understanding of the love to which Paul refers.

- *For even though I am absent in body, yet I am with you in spirit, rejoicing to see your good order and* <u>*the firmness*</u> **of your faith in Christ.** (Colossians 2:5, ESV). Here the prepositional phrase ("of your faith in Christ") tells us the type of firmness to which Paul refers.

- *For as* <u>*the body*</u> **without the spirit** *is dead, so* <u>*faith*</u> **without works** *is dead also.* (James 2:26, NKJV). Here the adjectival prepositional phrase is essential to the meaning. We need to know that it is faith "without works" that is being compared to a "body without the spirit" (a dead body).

Infinitive Phrases

Infinitive phrases can also follow noun heads and describe them.

- *God had not yet sent any rain, and there was* <u>*no one*</u> **to work the land***.* (Genesis 2:5b, CEV). The infinitive phrase "to work the land" describes what is meant by "no one."

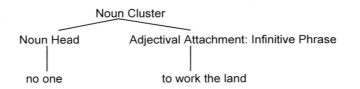

- *Whenever* <u>*the day*</u> *came* **for Elkanah to sacrifice***, he would give portions of the meat to his wife Peninnah and to all her sons and daughters.* (1 Samuel 1:4, NIV). In this verse, the verb comes between the head and the adjectival infinitive. This is a stylistic arrangement. In Edited American English, we would say, "the day for Elkanah to sacrifice came." Notice how the adjective phrase here explains the head. It was not simply "the day" but was "the day for Elkanah to sacrifice." We need the descriptive modifier to understand what day it is.

Relative Clauses

Relative clauses are adjectival statements that begin with a word known as a relative pronoun (*that, who, which, whose, whom, whoever, whomever*); they give more information about the noun head. Relative clauses follow the head that they describe. Recognizing the relative clause as adjectival and recognizing its attachment to its head are crucial to understanding the significance of this adjectival structure. In the Scriptures in English, relative clauses are plentiful.

- <u>*He*</u> **who criticizes a brother or judges his brother** *criticizes the law and judges the law.* (James 4:11, HCSB). You can see how important the relative clause is here. It is not merely "he" who speaks against the law and judges it; it is "he who criticizes a brother or judges his brother."

Noun Cluster

Noun Head   Adjectival Attachment: Relative Clause

he   who criticizes his brother or judges his brother

Missing Relative Pronoun   Sometimes there is a relative clause in a sentence, but the relative pronoun has been omitted. Recognizing this omission will help in understanding the role of the clause in the sentence.

- *For he has rescued us from the dominion of darkness and brought us into the kingdom of <u>the Son</u> **he loves, in whom we have redemption**, **the forgiveness of sins***. (Colossians 1:13-14, NIV). In this example, there are actually two relative clauses attached to the head "the Son." The second one, "in whom we have redemption," has the relative pronoun "whom." The first relative clause, "he loves" can be read as "[whom] he loves" with the addition of an ellipted "whom." Notice the noun appositive ("the forgiveness of sins") that renames "redemption." (See Chapter 5 for a further discussion of noun appositives.)
- *I will lead the blind by <u>a way</u> **they do not know**, in <u>paths</u> **they do not know** I will guide them*. (Isaiah 42:16a, NASB). Here the heads are "a way" and "paths," and the relative clause that describes them both is "[that] they do not know." Notice again how the relative clause adds important descriptive detail to the head. It is a significant task to lead blind people in a way that they do not know. This verse seems to refer to the spiritual blindness and resistance of the Israelites toward God.

In Chapter 8, we will continue to explore the meanings carried by relative clauses.

Participial Phrases

Participial phrases are phrases that begin with either an –*ing* (active participles) or an –*en* or –*ed* verb form (passive participles). Adjectival participial phrases generally come directly after the head but might also come directly before the head.

- *At his gate was laid <u>a beggar</u> **named Lazarus, covered with sores and longing to eat what fell from the rich man's table***. (Luke 16: 20-21, NIV). Here the head ("a beggar") is followed by three participial phrases ("named Lazarus," "covered with sores," and "longing to eat what fell from the rich man's table"). Notice that the participial phrases give added description and tell us more about the beggar.

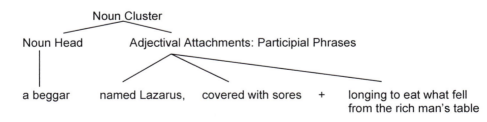

Noun Cluster

Noun Head   Adjectival Attachments: Participial Phrases

a beggar   named Lazarus,   covered with sores   +   longing to eat what fell
                                                            from the rich man's table

- *What is more, I consider everything <u>a loss</u>, **compared to the surpassing greatness of knowing Christ Jesus my Lord**, **for whose sake I have lost all things**. I consider them rubbish that I may gain Christ*. (Philippians 3:8, NIV). This participial phrase, "compared to the surpassing greatness of knowing Christ Jesus my Lord," adds important descriptive detail, explaining in what sense Paul thinks that everything he has mentioned is "a loss." These things are a loss by comparison with knowing Christ. Also notice that the relative clause ("for whose sake I have lost all things") attached to the head "Christ Jesus my Lord" adds descriptive detail.

- *Blessed is <u>the man that heareth me</u>, **watching daily at my gates**, **waiting at the posts of my doors**.* (Proverbs 8:34, NKJV). Notice the two participial phrases here: "watching daily at my gates," and "waiting at the posts of my doors." They describe "the man that heareth [God]." The head "the man that heareth me" has within it the relative clause "that heareth me" and the head of that clause is "the man." Notice that these adjectival modifiers add important descriptive detail.

Do not let the discussion of terms (such as *head*, *relative clause*, or *participial phrase*) cause you to become confused. What we are trying to do here is to find the <u>noun or noun cluster</u> and the <u>descriptive attachment</u>. Then we examine the meaning the descriptive attachment (the adjectives, prepositional phrases, infinitive phrase, relative clause, or participial phrase, for example) is adding to the head.

Significance of Adjectives in Bible Sentences

To Add Descriptive Detail
We have been looking at many examples of descriptive detail. Here is one more example, this one from a passage of poetry.

- *Bless <u>the LORD</u>, O my soul, and forget not all his benefits, **who forgives all your iniquity**, **who heals all your diseases**, **who redeems your life from the pit**, **who crowns you with steadfast love and mercy**, **who satisfies you with good so that your youth is renewed like the eagle's**.* (Psalm 103:2-5, ESV). All of these relative clauses describe the head "the Lord." Because these verses are from a passage of poetry, the sentence is written for poetic effect with the list of relative clauses describing the Lord at the end of the sentence rather than directly behind the head. This heightens the effect of the command "forget not all his benefits."

To Give Important Explanation and Instruction
Adjectival structures can also include important explanations and instructions, as well as descriptions. These adjectives are explanatory and essential to the meaning. The next example is from a piece of instructive literature.

- *Give your gifts in private, and <u>your Father</u>, **who sees everything**, will reward you.* (Matthew 6:4, NLT). This passage is from the Sermon on the Mount, in which Christ is teaching his followers how to live. Within this instructive literature, the relative clause has a clear purpose of explaining this attribute of God, which in turn explains why one should give in secret.

Another example of the use of adjectival structures for explanation can be found in the parable of the Prodigal Son:

- *"But when <u>this son of yours</u> came, **who has devoured your assets with prostitutes**, you slaughtered the fattened calf for him."* (Luke 15:30, HCSB). The relative clause in this verse serves the narrative literature by adding to the story. It explains why the older son does not understand his father's forgiveness: why would a father forgive such an immoral, disrespectful son? The descriptive detail of this relative clause also provides a contrast with the loving father, who responds in the next verses: *"Son,"* he said to him, *"you are always with me, and everything I have is yours. But we had to celebrate and rejoice, because this brother of yours was dead and is alive again; he was lost and is found."* (Luke 15:31-32, HCSB).

Questions for Analyzing Adjectival Structures

In summary, when trying to understand the significance of adjectival structures in Scripture, ask and answer these questions:

1. If the adjective follows a verb, it is a predicate adjective.
   - What is the subject?
   - What descriptive detail does the adjective structure add to the subject?
     - ✓ Remember always to find the complete predicate adjective to see the description of the subject.
     - ✓ Remember that the predicate adjective is not meant to describe all of the attributes of a subject fully.
     - ✓ Remember that a simile helps describe the subject by showing a similarity with another object.
2. If there are adjectives in front of a noun, what are they? What descriptive detail and meaning does the adjective add to the noun?
3. If the adjectival structure follows a noun, it is attached to a head.
   - What is the head?
   - What descriptive detail does the adjectival attachment add to the head?
   - How does the descriptive information help in understanding the passage?
4. What are the implications of the descriptive detail?

Some Practice

1 Peter 1:8

- *You love him even though you have never seen him. Though you do not see him now, you trust him; and you rejoice with a glorious, inexpressible joy.* (NLT).

In this passage, there are two adjectives in front of the noun "joy." They describe the joy that is found when one believes in Christ. It is not typical joy, but rather it is "glorious" and "inexpressible." The adjectives here add depth by describing the type and intensity of the joy found in Christ.

Philippians 1:24

- *But it is more necessary for you that I remain in the body.* (NIV).

Because this sentence is extraposed (see Chapter 3), the logical subject is the nominal clause "that I remain in the body," which is described by the predicate adjective "more necessary for you." The qualifier "more" goes with the adjective "necessary." Completing the adjective is the prepositional phrase "for you." Paul is not merely saying that his remaining in the body is necessary; rather, he is specifically saying that it is necessary *for you.*

Romans 3:14-15

- *Whose mouth is full of cursing and bitterness: Their feet are swift to shed blood.* (ASV).

In these two sentences, the adjectival structures come after the linking verbs, making them predicate adjectives. In the first sentence, the adjective "full" is completed by a prepositional phrase "of cursing and bitterness." The adjective "swift" in the second sentence is completed by an infinitive phrase describing how they were swift (swift "to shed blood"). These verses illustrate how essential it is to have a complete adjective. Being full of cursing and bitterness is very different from being full, and being swift to shed blood is very different from being merely swift.

Isaiah 58:11

- *You will be like a garden that has much water, like a spring that never runs dry.* (NLT).

This passage makes use of predicate adjectives that are similes. The context of the passage tells us that the "you" subject is people who cry out to God and who help the hungry and afflicted. In the two similes, they are being compared to a garden and a spring. "Garden" is further described by the relative clause "that has much water," and further description of the spring is added by the relative clause "that never runs dry." These relative clauses are important to the description because they tell us the type of garden and the type of spring to which the people are being compared. The image of abundant water is important to imply a richness of life.

Ephesians 1:13b-14

- *Having believed, you were marked in him with a seal, the promised Holy Spirit, who is a deposit guaranteeing our inheritance until the redemption of those who are God's possession – to the praise of His glory.* (NIV).

Here we start with an active participle phrase ("having believed"), which describes the subject "you." This participle phrase is absolutely essential because it explains the reason that we have the Holy Spirit. Also in this verse is a relative clause to tell more about the Holy Spirit, showing that the Holy Spirit, who is the seal of our salvation, is also a deposit of God's grace to us until the fullness of His grace can be shown for eternity. Also, notice in this verse that there is a noun appositive ("the promised Holy Spirit"), which defines the seal. (See Chapter 5 for a review of noun appositives.)

Daniel 2:22

- *It is He who reveals the profound and hidden things.* (NASB).

This is an extraposed sentence. (See Chapter 3 for a review of extraposed sentences.) A relative clause ("who reveals the profound and hidden things") comes after its head "he." It is necessary because it adds further detail to the noun, "he." Since "he" in the context of this verse is God, the relative clause explains to us something about God. Within the relative clause is a compound adjective that comes in front of the noun "things." "Profound" and "hidden" are both two very different adjectives that describe "things" and give us a better idea of their nature. These adjectives imply that God sees great things that we cannot and that he has authority and grace to reveal them.

Chapter 8
Adjectival Clauses and Phrases

Relative clauses and participial phrases are adjectival structures (modifiers) and therefore we looked at them briefly in Chapter 7. However, these modifiers, particularly relative clauses, appear so frequently in our English versions of the Bible that they merit more attention.

Analyzing Adjectival Clauses and Phrases

What is the Head?

As we saw in Chapter 7, the first necessary step towards understanding the implications of these adjectival structures in Scripture is to identify the head. This head will be a noun cluster or a pronoun. This is what the adjectival structure is describing or further identifying for us. In the two examples which follow, notice how the relative clauses (in bold) add descriptive detail to the heads (underlined).

- *Such teachings come from <u>the false words of liars</u> **whose consciences are destroyed as if by a hot iron**. They forbid people to marry and tell them not to eat <u>certain foods</u> **which God created to be eaten with thanks by <u>people</u> who believe and know the truth**.* (1 Timothy 4:2-3, NCV). The first relative clause adds descriptive detail to the head "the false words of liars." The second relative clause adds descriptive detail to the head "certain foods." Notice that in this second relative clause is imbedded a third clause adding detail to the head "people."

- *He has an unhealthy interest in controversies and quarrels about words that result in envy, strife, malicious talk, evil suspicions and constant friction between <u>men of corrupt mind</u>, **who have been robbed of the truth** and **who think that godliness is a means to financial gain**.* (1 Timothy 6:4b-5, NIV). These relative clauses give us particular insight into the men with corrupt minds by helping us understand what makes them corrupt.

Relative clauses are used in all types of writing to provide further information about a particular noun or noun cluster; however, any passage that contains a relative clause of which God is the head may have especially significant theological implications. These relative clauses help us to understand something about God.

- *Blessed be <u>the God and Father of our Lord Jesus Christ</u>, **who has blessed us with every spiritual blessing in the heavenly places in Christ**.* (Ephesians 1:3, NKJV). The head here is "the God and Father of our Lord Jesus Christ." The relative clause describes an attribute of God's grace, namely that he has blessed us spiritually. The adjectival structure here gives us important descriptive detail about God.

- *Now may our Lord Jesus Christ Himself, and our <u>God and Father</u>, **who has loved us and given us everlasting consolation and good hope by grace**, comfort your hearts and establish you in every good word and work.* (2 Thessalonians 2:16, NIV). This verse declares all of the good things that we have from God. We can be secure in God's love for us, delight in his grace, and boldly face the future with his eternal encouragement and good hope in our hearts. This verse is also interesting in that it could have either a singular head ("our God and Father") or a compound head (including "our Lord Jesus Christ Himself"). Notice the different theological implications of this – whether they should be referred to as one being or as separate.

Sometimes it may be a bit difficult to determine the head. For example, usually the modifier is "touching" the head, either directly before it or directly after it. However, in some versions of the Bible, translators are trying to follow the form of the original language as much as possible. In these cases, the modifier might not be touching the head. In the examples below, the relative clauses (in bold) do not directly follow the head. Therefore, we must find the head to determine the meaning and the implications.

- *For <u>we</u> are the true circumcision, **who worship in the Spirit of God and glory in Christ Jesus and put no confidence in the flesh***. (Philippians 3:3, NASB). In Edited American English, we would say, "For we who worship in the Spirit of God and glory in Christ Jesus and put no confidence in the flesh are the true circumcision."

- *The sorrows of <u>those</u> will increase **who run after other gods***. (Psalm 16:4, NIV). The sentence here has been scrambled a bit from the normal order. We would normally say, "The sorrows of those who run after other gods will increase." It is important to determine the head ("those") so that we can attach "who run after other gods" to determine whose sorrows will increase.

- *And then <u>the lawless one</u> will be revealed **whom the Lord will consume with the breath of His mouth and destroy with the brightness of His coming***. (2 Thessalonians 2:8, NKJV). This is another example of a sentence that deviates from Edited American English in that the relative clause should come directly after "the lawless one" but instead comes at the end. It is "the lawless one" whom the Lord will "consume."

- *And even as they did not like to retain God in their knowledge, God gave them over to <u>a debased mind</u>, to do those things which are not fitting; **being filled with all unrighteousness, sexual immorality, wickedness, covetousness, maliciousness; full of envy, murder, strife, deceit, evil-mindedness***. (Romans 1:28-29, NKJV). Notice that the two long adjectival modifiers beginning with "being" and with "full" describe the head ("a debased mind"). These adjective structures give us a good description of what a debased mind is like. However, they do not come directly before or after the head, as they would in Edited American English.

- *And he made known to us <u>the mystery of his will</u> according to his good pleasure, **which he purposed in Christ***. (Ephesians 1:9, NIV). In this case, "the mystery of God's will" is the head, and the relative clause tells us that the central figure of this "mystery of his will" is Christ. God sent Christ to earth to fulfill his will. "According to his good pleasure" is another adjectival structure (in this case, a prepositional phrase) describing his will.

Is the Modifier Restrictive or Nonrestrictive?

The meaning of a Bible sentence might depend upon whether the modifier is **restrictive** or **nonrestrictive**. Relative clauses and participial phrases can be either restrictive or nonrestrictive. Both types modify or describe the head, but restrictive modifiers restrict or limit the definition of the head to which they are attached. Restrictive modifiers are needed to understand the head correctly. Nonrestrictive modifiers merely add information to the head.

Nonrestrictive modifiers are set off by commas or dashes; restrictive modifiers are not set off by punctuation. We must, of course, trust that the translators have punctuated correctly and therefore are correctly signaling whether the relative clause or participial phrase is restrictive or not.

Whether a modifier is restrictive or is nonrestrictive can definitely affect the meaning. In fact, noticing whether the modifier is restrictive can be vital to the meaning.

Restrictive Modifiers

Remember that restrictive clauses and phrases are not separated from their head by any marks of punctuation. These adjectival structures restrict or limit the definition of the head to which they are attached.

- *<u>The one</u> **who speaks against a brother or judges his brother** speaks evil against the law and judges the law*. (James 4:11b, ESV). This statement is a good example of what a restrictive relative clause does. Without it, this statement would be unclear, saying "<u>the one</u> judges the law." However, the restrictive relative clause narrows, or restricts, the head ("the one") so that the statement is clear in its intended subject. It is not merely "the one" but "the one who speaks against a brother or judges his brother."

- *You, therefore, have no excuse, <u>you</u> **who pass judgment on someone else**, for at whatever point you judge the other, you are condemning yourself, because you **who pass judgment** do the same things.* (Romans 2:1, NIV). Paul uses relative clauses here to clarify for whom this warning is intended. The head is "you"; Paul is addressing readers directly, but the relative clause is restrictive because it indicates which readers he is addressing specifically. He is talking to "you who pass judgment on someone else."

- *But I say to you, love your enemies; bless <u>those</u> **who curse you**. Do good to <u>those</u> **who hate you**, and pray for <u>those</u> **who spitefully use you and persecute you**.* (Matthew 5:44, NKJV). In this statement from the Sermon on the Mount, the restrictive relative clause tells the audience which of "those" (the head) we should bless: those who curse you, those who hate you, and those who spitefully use and persecute you. The relative clause is restrictive because it significantly narrows which people Jesus is talking about in this statement.

- *The LORD is always kind to <u>those</u> **who worship him**, and he keeps his promises to <u>their descendants</u> **who faithfully obey him**.* (Psalm 103:17-18, CEV). The restrictive clauses in this passage describe the attributes of "those," the head. These attributes, however, do not merely add descriptive detail; they also restrict the head by indicating which of "those" the author is describing. He is talking about a specific group, and the modifier is necessary so that we know exactly who is in the group. The second restrictive relative clause is particularly interesting. The Lord keeps his promises to their descendants who faithfully obey him. No promise is made to descendants who do not faithfully obey.

- *Therefore, get rid of all moral filth and the evil that is so prevalent and humbly accept <u>the word</u> **planted in you, which can save you**.* (James 1:21, NIV). The head ("the word") has both a passive participial phrase and a relative clause attached to it. The passive participial phrase "planted in you" is restrictive because it is necessary for understanding the head, "the word." What "word" do we mean here? It is the word "planted in you." On the other hand, the relative clause is nonrestrictive, set off by a comma, but it adds descriptive detail to the head. The relative clause tells us that the word can save us. Of course, we also need to know that the referent or antecedent for the pronoun "you" is the Christians to whom James is writing. (See Chapter 6 for a discussion of antecedents.)

- *For when <u>Gentiles</u> **who do not have the Law** do instinctively the things of the Law, these, not having the Law, are a law to themselves, in that they show the work of <u>the Law</u> **written in their hearts**.* (Romans 2:14-15, NASB). The first relative clause ("who do not have the Law") defines for us the subject and restricts it to Gentiles who do not have the Law. The participial phrase "written in their hearts" restricts the meaning of "the Law" to just that which is written in their hearts. Understanding that these two relative clauses are restrictive and therefore restrict (define) the heads is crucial to understanding the meaning.

- *Since you have heard about Jesus and have learned <u>the truth</u> **that comes from him**, throw off your old sinful nature and <u>your former way of life</u>, **which is corrupted by lust and deception**.* (Ephesians 4:21-22, NLT). Without the restrictive relative clause, we might ask "what truth?" The answer is the truth that comes from Jesus. This verse points to the source of truth: God, and more specifically, Jesus. The second relative clause ("which is corrupted by lust and deception") is nonrestrictive; it does not specifically define the former way of life; it adds detail.

Nonrestrictive Modifiers

Nonrestrictive clauses and phrases give more information about the head. They are set off with punctuation such as commas or sometimes dashes.

- *With it we bless our Lord and Father, and with it we curse* <u>men</u>*, **who have been made in the likeness of God**.* (James 3:9, NASB). While this relative clause is certainly crucial to the meaning of the passage, it is nonrestrictive because it does not restrict or narrow the head, which is "men." "Men" here refers to all people, who have all been made in God's likeness. The information in the relative clause is given as additional information about the head as opposed to information necessary to understand the definition of the head. The implication of the clause being nonrestrictive is that all people have been made in the likeness of God.

- *Bless* <u>the LORD</u>*, O my soul, and forget not all His benefits: **who forgives all your iniquities**, **who heals all your diseases**, **who redeems your life from destruction, who crowns you with lovingkindness and tender mercies**, **who satisfies your mouth with good things**, **so that your youth is renewed like the eagle's**.* (Psalm 103:2-5, NKJV). In this poetic passage, the series of three relative clauses adds information to the head, "the Lord." In a sense, one could consider "his benefits" to also be a head, since the "*his*" refers to the Lord. The passage as a whole is a description of the Lord, and the relative clauses are descriptive (or nonrestrictive) rather than restrictive. We do not need the relative clause to tell us <u>which</u> Lord is meant.

- *The kingdom of heaven is like* <u>a mustard seed</u>*, **which a man took and sowed in his field**.* (Matthew 13:31b, NKJV). The nonrestrictive relative clause adds additional information to the head, "a mustard seed," but it does not restrict the head. Note that the phrase "like a mustard seed" signals a simile, a comparison of two otherwise unlike items (see Chapter 7).

- *Blessed is* <u>the one **who listens to me**</u>*, **watching daily at my gates**, **waiting beside my doors**.* (Proverbs 8:34, ESV). The relative clause "who listens to me" is restrictive. It is necessary to know which "one" is blessed. However, the two participial phrases ("watching daily at my gates" and "waiting beside my doors") are nonrestrictive, giving more descriptive detail about the man who listens.

- *The LORD, the LORD,* <u>the compassionate and gracious God</u>*, **slow to anger, abounding in love and faithfulness**, **maintaining love to thousands**, and **forgiving wickedness, rebellion and sin**.* (Exodus 34:6-7, NIV). This passage contains three adjectival participial phrases, all of which give additional information about their common head, "God." They are all nonrestrictive, because the head—God—needs no further definition. The phrase "slow to anger" is an adjectival appositive, which also gives additional descriptive detail (see Chapter 7).

- *But there was* <u>a certain beggar</u> ***named Lazarus, full of sores, who was laid at his gate, desiring to be fed with*** <u>the crumbs</u> ***which fell from the rich man's table***.* (Luke 16: 20-21a, NKJV). The head "a certain beggar" has four attachments. The first ("named Lazarus") is restrictive, defining the beggar as a specific man. The second three ("full of sores," "who was laid at his gate" and "desiring to be fed with the crumbs which fell from the rich man's table") do not restrict the head but instead provide additional descriptive detail. There is another head in this sentence – "the crumbs" to which a restrictive relative clause ("which fell from the rich man's table") is attached. Here, "the crumbs" is restricted to those particular crumbs that came from the rich man's table. The relative clause identifies which crumbs.

- *For we are* <u>His creation</u>*—**created in Christ Jesus for** <u>good works</u>*, **which God prepared ahead of time so that we should walk in them**.* (Ephesians 2:10, HCSB). In this verse, the verb "are" is a linking verb joining the subject "we" to the predicate nominative "his creation." Predicate nominatives rename the subject, so "we" and "his creation" refer to the same thing (see Chapter 5). So, while "his creation" is the actual head, the nonrestrictive participial phrase refers to both "his creation" and "we." It tells us more information about the head, saying that we (the author is talking about followers of Christ) were created to do good works. While we do not need the phrase to define the head, it gives enriching detail. That is what a nonrestrictive adjectival phrase does. There is also a relative clause in this verse. The relative clause ("which God prepared ahead of time so that we should walk in them") is also nonrestrictive. It adds descriptive detail to its head "good works."

It is important for us to remember that we are dependent upon the skill of the translator to punctuate the Bible sentences correctly since, in this case, punctuation signals whether a clause or phrase is restrictive or nonrestrictive, and that, as we have seen above, can distinctly affect the meaning.

Significance of Adjectival Clauses and Phrases in Scripture

Adjectival modifiers are very important in Scripture. When we see an adjectival modifier, we should examine it closely to see how it is functioning. The discussion that follows illustrates four of the possible purposes for adjectival clauses and phrases in the Bible.

To Clarify Identification

One purpose for adjectival modifiers in Scripture is to clarify and help identify the head. Notice in the following examples that the relative clause (in bold) clarifies the identification of the head (underlined).

- *Then came to him all his brothers and sisters and <u>all</u> **who had know him before**, and ate bread with him in his house. And they showed him sympathy and comforted him for <u>all the evil</u> **that the LORD had brought upon him**.* (Job 42:11, ESV). The relative clauses clarify who "all" were and help explain the background to "all the evil."
- *This took place after he had defeated <u>King Sihon of the Amorites</u>, **who had ruled in Heshbon**, and <u>King Og of Bashan</u>, **who had ruled in Ashtaroth and Edrei**.* (Deuteronomy 1:4, NLT). The relative clauses provide information about the locations from which Sihon and Og ruled their respective territories. In each clause, the relative pronoun "who" helps identify the particular king.
- *See, I have given you this land. Go in and take possession of <u>the land</u> **that the LORD swore he would give to your fathers—to Abraham, Isaac, and Jacob—and to their descendants after them**.* (Deuteronomy 1:8, NIV). In this verse, "I" refers to God. The relative clause refers to the land of Canaan. This relative clause clarifies that the land was given to the descendants of Abraham, Isaac and Jacob.
- *The sorrows of <u>those</u> will increase **who run after other gods**.* (Psalm 16:4, NIV). The sentence here has been scrambled a bit from the normal order. We would normally say, "The sorrows of those who run after other gods will increase." The relative clause serves to specify whose sorrows will increase: people who deny God's authority and sovereignty.
- *Behold, bless the LORD, <u>all servants of the LORD</u>, **who serve by night in the house of the LORD**.* (Psalm 134:1, NASB). The relative clause again clarifies the identification. The servants of the Lord in this verse are the Levites, who were responsible for the functioning and maintenance of the temple both day and night. This verse is an exhortation to the Levites to praise the Lord as they worked in his temple.
- *<u>He</u> **who walks righteously and speak uprightly, who despises the pain of oppressions, who shakes his hands, lest they hold a bribe, who stops his ears from hearing of bloodshed and shuts his eyes from looking on evil**, he will dwell on the heights; his place of defense will be the fortresses of rocks; his break will be given him; his water will be sure.* (Isaiah 33:15-16, ESV). These verses are about the man who pleases God and the rewards and security that are his. The relative clauses clarify "he" by supplying specific details regarding actions that honor God. A man who does these things will find his protection and provision in God.

- *Blessings on* the one **who comes in the name of the LORD**! (Matthew 21:9b, NLT). The relative clause helps to describe the person who will be blessed. Notice the ellipsis in the sentence as well. (See Chapter 3 for a review of ellipsis.)

To Describe Abstract Terms

Modifiers are also used in Scripture to help explain abstract terms such as *love* or *faith* by giving more information about them.

- *...and to know* the Messiah's love **that surpasses knowledge,** *so you may be filled with all the fullness of God.* (Ephesians 3:19, HCSB). This relative clause explains that with our limited human minds, we cannot comprehend God's love fully.
- *Since you have heard about Jesus and have learned* the truth **that comes from him,** *throw off* your old sinful nature and your former way of life, **which is corrupted by lust and deception.** (Ephesians 4:21-22, NLT). The first relative clause describes the truth, reminding us that it comes from Christ. The second helps explain "your old sinful nature and your former way of life." People who do not know Christ but live to gratify the desires of the sinful nature are being corrupted.
- *In all circumstances take up* the shield of faith, **with which you can extinguish all the flaming darts of the evil one.** (Ephesians 6:16, ESV). In this case, the relative clause details the uses of its head, "the shield of faith." Therefore, the modifier gives some information about the abstract term. Growing and becoming strong in faith is essential for Christians so that we can fully trust God and not be injured by the lies and schemes that Satan sends our way.
- *And take the helmet of salvation, and* the sword of the Spirit, **which is the word of God.** (Ephesians 6:17, ASV). The relative clause defines its abstract head in this verse. The sword of the Spirit is the word of God.
- *And* the peace of God, **which surpasses all comprehension,** *will guard your hearts and your minds in Christ Jesus.* (Philippians 4:7, NASB). The head of the relative clause is "the peace of God"; the relative clause tells how vast and powerful this peace is; it cannot be intellectually grasped or analyzed, but it exists as a serenity of the soul that cannot be completely understood or explained.

To Explain and Teach

Sometimes the modifier adds detail that is important to explain something and to teach us.

- *The LORD swore to David* a sure oath **from which he will not turn back:** *"One of the sons of your body I will set on your throne."* (Psalm 132:11, ESV). In this verse, the relative clause teaches us about God's oaths, in this case, an oath made to David. It was an oath that God would keep.
- *In that day the Egyptians will be like women. They will shudder with fear at* the uplifted hand **that the LORD Almighty raises against them.** (Isaiah 19:16, NIV). This verse paints a picture of God bringing his wrath upon the people of Egypt. The relative clause teaches us that it is the Lord Almighty who is bringing judgment upon them.
- *But evil people are like* the angry sea, **which cannot rest, whose waves toss up waste and mud.** (Isaiah 57:20, NCV). This verse has a prepositional phrase predicate adjective (see Chapter 7), which describes the wicked as being like the sea. The relative clauses explain to us which characteristics of a tossing sea are applicable to the wicked.
- *According to* the eternal purpose **which he purposed in** Christ Jesus our Lord: **In whom we have boldness and access with confidence by the faith of him.** (Ephesians 3:11, KJV). The first relative clause here teaches us something about the eternal purpose of God: it was accomplished in Christ Jesus. The second relative clause further teaches us about the boldness and access we have through him.

- *And then* <u>*the lawless one*</u> *will be revealed,* **whom the Lord will consume with the breath of His mouth and destroy with the brightness of His coming**. (2 Thessalonians 2:8, NKJV). This is another example of a sentence that deviates from Edited American English in that the relative clause is separated from its head by the verb. Nonetheless, we can see that the relative clause teaches us something about Satan, the lawless one: Satan will be overthrown. Whereas the head of this relative clause is "the lawless one," his importance in this verse is secondary to that of Jesus. For Jesus to show up and to breathe on the lawless one is enough to fell him, demonstrating the superiority of Jesus' power.

- *For this reason we also thank God without ceasing, because when you received* <u>*the word of God*</u> **which you heard from us**, *you welcomed it not as the word of men, but as it is in truth,* <u>*the word of God*</u>, **which also effectively works in you who believe**. (1 Thessalonians 2:13, NKJV). This verse has two relative clauses that teach us about the word of God. Paul had spoken the word of God to them, and God's word, living and active (Hebrews 4:12), is working in all Christians who truly believe.

To Describe God

Relative clauses can be particularly important in giving us descriptive detail about God. The first set of examples has relative clauses telling us about God, the Lord.

- *In* <u>*Him*</u> *also we have obtained an inheritance, having been predestined according to His purpose* **who works all things after the counsel of His will,** *to the end that we who were the first to hope in Christ would be to the praise of His glory.* (Ephesians 1:10b-12, NASB). The pronoun "him" in this verse refers to God, and it is the head of the relative clause. (Notice how far separated the relative clause is from the head). The relative clause provides Christians with the assurance that God is sovereign. There is a second relative clause in this sentence that later describes us.

- *Oh, let the evil of the wicked come to an end, and may you establish the righteous—*<u>*you*</u> **who test the minds and hearts,** *O righteous God!* (Psalm 7:9, ESV). The relative clause conveys the concept of God's omniscience and his ability to know our minds and hearts by testing, trying, and searching them.

- *For I am* <u>*the LORD, your God*</u>, **who takes hold of your right hand and says to you,** "**Do not fear; I will help you.**" (Isaiah 41:13, NIV). The context of this verse is God speaking to Israel. It declares the gentle yet powerful nature of God. He is the God that stands by our side and holds our hand when we are facing hard times. He tells us not to fear because he will help us.

- *This is what* <u>*God the LORD*</u> *says—***who created the heavens and stretched them out, who spread out the earth and what comes from it, who gives breath to the people on it and life to those who walk on it** — (Isaiah 42:5, HCSB). The relative clauses in this verse testify to the power of God and His responsibility in creating and sustaining life on earth. He made the heavens, the earth, and everything on the earth. He is the source of life.

- *This is what* <u>*the Lord*</u>, **who saves you,** *the Holy One of Israel, says:* "*I am* <u>*the Lord your God*</u>, **who teaches you to do what is good, who leads you in the way you should go**." (Isaiah 48:17, NCV). Here are more relative clauses that describe God. God is the one who saves us. He can also be trusted to lead and guide his people in the way that He wants them to go, which is best for them.

- *...giving thanks to* <u>*the Father*</u>, **who has qualified you to share in the inheritance of the saints in the kingdom of light**. (Colossians 1:12, NIV). *Praise be to* <u>*the God and Father of our Lord Jesus Christ*</u>, **who has blessed us in the heavenly realms with every spiritual blessing in Christ**. (Ephesians 1:3, NIV). The relative clauses in these two verses tell us some of what God has made available to us. As Christians, we are blessed by God and are recipients, through our relationship with him, of a spiritual inheritance and every spiritual blessing.

There are also relative clauses that teach us more about Jesus Christ.

- *Grace to you and peace from God our Father and* <u>*the Lord Jesus Christ*</u>*,* **who gave Himself for our sins so that He might rescue us from this present evil age,** *according to the will of* <u>*our God and Father*</u>*,* **to whom be the glory forevermore.** *Amen.* (Galatians 1:3-4, NASB). The first relative clause explains how we obtained the grace and peace from God. From it we can learn Jesus' role in God's will. His role was to be sacrificed on our behalf, making a relationship with God possible. The second relative clause refers to "our God and Father."

- *I have died, but Christ lives in me. And I now live by faith in* <u>*the Son of God*</u>*,* **who loved me and gave his life for me**. (Galatians 2:20, CEV). In this instance, the relative clause about Jesus teaches us about his sacrificial love.

- *So you also are complete through your union with* <u>*Christ*</u>*,* **who is the head over every ruler and authority**. (Colossians 2:10, NLT). The relative clause describes Christ and his power and place in the world. His greatness and position as head over all makes the fullness we have in him even more significant.

- *I can do all things through* <u>*Christ*</u> **who strengthens me**. (Philippians 4:13, NKJV). The relative clause teaches that we can have confidence knowing that Christ is the source of our strength and abilities. Relying on ourselves becomes hopeless when we know that only through Christ can we find our endurance.

Some relative clauses explain more about the effects of the death and resurrection of Christ.

- *But God forbid that I should glory, save in* <u>*the cross of our Lord Jesus Christ*</u>*,* **by whom the world is crucified unto me, and I unto the world**. (Galatians 6:14, KJV). In this particular case, the relative clause is modifying "the cross of our Lord Jesus Christ." This cross is the means by which Christ conquered sin, Satan, and death. Because of his victory on the cross, we no longer need to be conformed to the world (Romans 12).

- *to the praise of* <u>*His glorious grace*</u>*,* **which he has freely given us in** <u>*the One*</u> *he loves*. (Ephesians 1:6, NIV). The relative clause explains that through Christ ("the One [that] he loves"), we have the grace of God. We are the beneficiaries of God's grace and not of His wrath because Christ paid the penalty for our sins. Christ, the One (that) God loves, made the gift of grace possible.

- *For He rescued us from the domain of darkness, and transferred us to the kingdom of* <u>*His beloved Son*</u>*,* **in whom we have redemption, the forgiveness of sins**. (Colossians 1:13-14, NASB). The relative clause tells us that it is through Jesus that we have been forgiven and given redemption.

- *This is according to* <u>*the purpose of the ages*</u>*,* **which He made in** <u>*the Messiah, Jesus our Lord*</u>*,* **in whom we have boldness, access, and confidence through faith in Him**. (Ephesians 3:11-12, HCSB). We have access to God—bold, confident access—because of Jesus.

Finally, we also learn of the Holy Spirit through relative clauses.

- *In* <u>*Him*</u> *you also trusted, after you heard the word of truth, the gospel of your salvation;* **in whom also,** *having believed,* **you were sealed with** <u>*the Holy Spirit of promise*</u>*,* **who is the guarantee of our inheritance until the redemption of the purchased possession, to the praise of His glory**. (Ephesians 1:13-14, NKJV). Here the head of the first relative clause is "him," referring to Jesus Christ. "The Holy Spirit of promise" is the head for the second relative clause, which provides further description and details regarding the Spirit.

- *And do not grieve* <u>*the Holy Spirit of God*</u>*,* **by whom you were sealed for the day of redemption**. (Ephesians 4:30, ESV). A seal in those times showed ownership. The presence of the Holy Spirit in a Christian is God's sign of ownership.

Questions for Analyzing Adjectival Clauses and Phrases

In summary, when trying to understand the significance of adjectival clauses and phrases in Scripture, ask and answer these questions:

1. What is the head?
2. Is the relative clause or participial phrase restrictive or nonrestrictive? (Check the punctuation.) What does this imply for the meaning?
3. What descriptive detail does the adjectival modifier add to the head?
4. How does the descriptive information help in understanding the passage?
   - Does the adjectival modifier clarify identification?
   - Does the adjectival modifier describe an abstract term?
   - Does the adjectival modifier explain and teach?
   - Does the adjectival modifier tell us more about God?

Some Practice

Proverbs 31:30

- *Charm is deceitful and beauty is passing, but* <u>a woman</u> **who fears the LORD,** *she shall be praised.* (NKJV).

This is an example of a restrictive relative clause in which the fact that it is restrictive is important to the meaning. Not just any woman but rather she who fears the Lord is to be praised.

Romans 8:32

- <u>He</u> **who did not spare his own Son, but gave him up for us all**—*how will he not also, along with him, graciously give us all things?* (NIV).

It is interesting when relative clauses that refer to God are restrictive. The punctuation here indicates that the relative clause ("who...for us all") is restrictive, although we know that God does not need any clarification. However, this modifier is telling an essential element of God for Christians and prevents the ambiguity that would be present without the clause. For us, God's act of giving up his son for us all is not just another thing that God did, as a nonrestrictive clause might imply; rather, it is the key to our salvation. Paul is also trying to explain that God is a generous God who is willing and able to give us what we need. The relative clause explains just how willing and able he really is—that he must intend to give us all things if he already gave us what is most valuable to him: his son. Furthermore, in the Greek New Testament, this verse does not begin with "he"; instead, the nominal clause "who did not spare his own Son" stands alone, almost acting as a name of God. When translated, the addition of the "he" made it easier to read, while leaving out punctuation after the "he" still gave the idea that the whole phrase "he who did not spare his own Son" was working as a single unit.

Romans 4:17

Because it can change the meaning, the punctuation signaling a restrictive or nonrestrictive modifier could be verified by using different translations. Romans 4:17 in the NIV makes the relative clause restrictive even though the head (God) does not seem to need clarification. The New Living Translation and the New Century Version follow a similar pattern.

- *[Abraham] is our father in the sight of God, in whom he believed*—<u>the God</u> **who gives life to the dead and calls things that are not as though they were**. (NIV). This relative clause identifies God because it is restrictive. Perhaps the NIV translators made the clause restrictive to distinguish God from the gods whom the other people around Abraham worshipped.

However, the NASB assumes that God does not need to be further identified and so has the relative clause as nonrestrictive. This is similar to the punctuation in the Holman Christian Standard Bible, English Standard Version, and New King James Version.

- *As it is written, "A father of many nations have I made you" in the presence of Him whom he believed, even <u>God</u>, **who gives life to the dead and calls into being that which does not exist**.* (Romans 4:17, NASB).

Note that all of the versions give the same descriptive details about God.

Exodus 20:2

- *"I am <u>the Lord your God</u>, **who brought you out of the land of Egypt where you were slaves**."* (NCV).

The context of this verse is the time during which God gave the Ten Commandments to Moses. There is a nonrestrictive relative clause in this verse ("who brought you out of the land of Egypt where you were slaves"). It gives us more information about God. It is enough for his people to obey him just because he is the Lord, but God adds another description. He reminds them that he brought them out of slavery and is therefore even more deserving of their obedience.

Hebrews 12:1

- *Therefore, since we are surrounded by so great a cloud of witnesses, let us also lay aside every weight, and <u>sin</u> **which clings so closely**, and let us run with endurance <u>the race</u> **that is set before us**, looking to <u>Jesus, the founder and perfecter of our faith</u>, **who for the joy that was set before him endured the cross**, **despising the shame**, **and is seated at the right hand of the throne of God**.* (ESV).

The first relative clause "which clings so closely" is an example of a place where the reason for choosing a restrictive clause rather than a nonrestrictive one is not necessarily clear. It does not seem necessary to clarify that the author is talking about the "sin which clings so closely," because it seems clear from Scripture that all sin can easily entangle us. However, the fact that sin can easily entangle is such an intrinsic part of sin's nature that perhaps using a nonrestrictive clause does not emphasize its entangling nature enough.

The second relative clause is also restrictive, with "the race" acting as the head, further explained as the specific race "that is set before us." Finally, the head of "Jesus" is set off from a nonrestrictive relative clause that begins with "who" and continues until the end of the passage. Jesus is further described by the phrases but does not need to be defined by them. We learn much more about Jesus through the relative clause.

Acts 10:40-41

- *God raised Him up on the third day and granted that He become visible, not to all the people, but to <u>witnesses</u> **who were chosen beforehand by God**, that is, to <u>us</u> **who ate and drank with Him after He arose from the dead**.* (NASB).

This passage uses two relative clauses; both are restrictive. The first relative clause restricts the meaning of "witnesses" and leaves out anyone who was not chosen by God. The second relative clause defines the speakers as witnesses through certain actions – the eating and drinking with the risen Christ. These restrictive relative clauses are necessary to define the heads.

Chapter 9
Adverbial Structures

Questions that Adverbs Answer

Adverbs are words or groups of words that answer adverb questions. The adverbs in any given sentence will answer questions such as the ones listed below. The table that follows contains some adverb questions and their corresponding labels along with examples drawn from the Bible.

ADVERB QUESTION	ADVERB LABEL	EXAMPLE
How?	Adverb of Manner	*steadfastly* (2 Chronicles 27:6, NIV) *with endurance* (Hebrews 12:1, ESV) *boldly* (Ephesians 6:19-20, NLT)
When?	Adverb of Time	*in the beginning* (John 1:1, NLT) *on the Sabbath day* (Matthew 12:2, NCV) *when Peter saw this* (Acts 3:12, NCV)
Where?	Adverb of Place	*in the Jordan* (Matthew 3:6, NKJV) *on the Mount of Olives* (Matthew 24:3, NIV) *in the portico called Solomon's* (Acts 3:11, ESV)
Why?	Adverb of Reason	*because he prepared his ways before the LORD his God* (2 Chronicles 27:6, KJV) *for his name's sake* (Romans 1:5, NIV) *so that it spreads no further among the people* (Acts 4:17, NKJV)
Through what means?	Adverb of Means	*by the resurrection from the dead* (Romans 1:4, NKJV) *by word and deed* (Romans 15:18, ESV) *by grace* (Ephesians 2:8, NCV)
To what extent?	Adverb of Extent	*with all your heart* (Proverbs 3:5, NCV) *in all your ways* (Proverbs 3:6, NKJV) *to the heart* (Acts 2:37, NKJV)
How often?	Adverb of Frequency	*without ceasing* (1 Thessalonians 5:17, ASV) *always* (Philippians 4:4, HCSB) *daily* (Acts 2:47, NKJV)
How far?	Adverb of Distance	*about three or four miles* (John 6:19, ESV) *all the way to Jezreel* (1 Kings 18:46, NIV) *as far as the east is from the west* (Psalm 103:12, NASB)
Under what condition?	Adverb of Condition	*while Jesus was still speaking* (Luke 22:47, NCV) *even though I walk through the valley of the shadow of death* (Psalm 23:4, NIV) *though war arise against me* (Psalm 27:3, ESV)
To whom? To what?	Adverb of Recipient	*to Joseph* (Mark 15:45, KJV) *to the poor* (Matthew 26:9, NLT) *for the good of those who love him* (Romans 8:28, NIV)
How long?	Adverb of Duration	*until he [the Lord] comes and showers righteousness on you* (Hosea 10:12, NIV) *from the beginning of creation* (Romans 1:20, CEV) *each day of my life* (Psalm 23:6, CEV)

ADVERB QUESTION	ADVERB LABEL	EXAMPLE
With what instrument?	Adverb of Instrument	*with water* (Matthew 3:11, NLT) *with the Holy Spirit and with fire* (Matthew 3:11, NLT) *with rods* (2 Corinthians 11:25, ESV)
By whom?	Adverb of Agency	*by Him* (Colossians 1:16, NASB) *by God* (Isaiah 53:4, NIV) *by them* (Deuteronomy 7:21, NIV)
With whom?	Adverb of Association	*with God* (John 1:1, NLT) *with them* (Matthew 26:36, ESV) *with each other* (1 John 1:7, NLT)
From where?	Adverb of Origin	*among all the Gentiles* (Romans 1:5, NASB) *from Jerusalem and all Judea and the whole region of the Jordan* (Matthew 3:5, NIV) *from Tiberias* (John 6:23, NCV)
From whom or what?	Adverb of Source	*from me* (Genesis 2:23, CEV) *from the Father of lights* (James 1:17, NKJV) *from her* (Genesis 17:16, NLT)
In what order?	Adverb of Order	*before the rooster crows tomorrow morning* (Luke 22:34, NLT) *first* (Genesis 25:31, NIV) *last of all* (Genesis 33:2, ESV)
Compared to what?	Adverb of Comparison	*More highly than he ought to think* (Romans 12:3, RSV) *in comparison* (Haggai 2:3, NASB) *much harder...more frequently...more severely* (2 Corinthians 11:23, NIV)
To where?	Adverb of Destination	*into the wilderness* (Matthew 4:1, NASB) *to the Jordan* (Judges 8:4, NASB) *to Siloam* (John 9:11, NCV)
In what direction?	Adverb of Direction	*away* (Matthew 24:1, ESV) *on the right side of the boat* (John 21:6, NIV) *on his right and ...on his left* (Matthew 27:38, NASB)
How near or far?	Adverb of Proximity	*nearby* (John 19:42, NKJV) *as far as Sodom* (Genesis 13:12, ESV) *in the distance* (Genesis 37:18, NIV)

Recognizing Adverbs

Adverbs can be a single word.

- *See that no one renders evil for evil to anyone, but **always** pursue what is good both for yourselves and for all.* (1 Thessalonians 5:15, NKJV). The adverb "always" answers the adverb question "to what extent?" or "how often?"

Often adverbs in English are prepositional phrases, infinitive phrases, or adverbial participial phrases.

- ***Then** Jesus was led **up by the Spirit into the wilderness to be tempted by the devil**.* (Matthew 4:1, NASB). There are several adverbs in this verse; actually, the only part that is not adverbial is "Jesus was led." The adverbs are shown in the table that follows.

Adverb Question	Adverb	Adverb Type
In what order?	*then*	single word
In what direction?	*up*	single word
By whom?	*by the Spirit*	prepositional phrase
To where?	*into the wilderness*	prepositional phrase
Why?	*to be tempted*	infinitive phrase
By whom?	*by the devil*	prepositional phrase

Sometimes an adverb is a noun cluster.

- *Surely goodness and loving kindness will follow me **all the days of my life**.* (Psalm 23:6a, NLT). The adverb phrase "all the days of my life" is a noun cluster that answers the adverb question "how long?"

Longer adverbs are subordinate clauses. An adverb clause will begin with a subordinating conjunction such as those below.

Words that Can Function as Subordinating Conjunctions										
after	*although*	*as*	*because*	*before*	*for*	*when*	*lest*	*once*	*provided*	*since*
until	*wherever*	*if*	*whenever*	*where*	*till*	*whether*	*while*	*unless*	*though*	

Words that Can Function as Cluster Subordinating Conjunctions					
as if	*as long as*	*as soon as*	*as though*	*even though*	*in as much as*
even if	*in order that*	*in so far as*	*no matter how*	*so that*	*whether or not*

- ***Even though I walk through the valley of the shadow of death**, I will fear no evil, **for you are with me**.* (Psalm 23:4a, NIV). The only part of the sentence that is not an adverb is "I will fear no evil."

Adverb Question	Adverb	Adverb Type
Under what conditions?	*even though I walk through the valley of the shadow of death*	adverb clause
Where?	*through the valley of the shadow of death*	prepositional phrase
Why?	*for you are with me*	adverb clause
With whom?	*with me*	prepositional phrase

- *But **when he saw the strength of the wind**, he was afraid. And **beginning to sink**, he cried out, "Lord, save me!"* (Matthew 14:30, HCSB).

Adverb Question	Adverb	Adverb Type
When?	*when he saw the strength of the wind*	adverb clause
Under what condition?	*beginning to sink*	active participial phrase

- ***Convinced of this**, I know that I will remain and continue **with you all**, **for your progress and joy in the faith**, **so that in me you may have ample cause to glory in Christ Jesus**, **because of my coming to you again**.* (Philippians 1:25, ESV). The adverbs are shown in the table that follows.

Adverb Question	Adverb	Adverb Type
How?	*convinced of this*	passive participial phrase
With whom?	*with you all*	prepositional phrase
Why?	*for your progress and joy in the faith*	prepositional phrase
Why?	*so that in me you may have ample cause to glory in Christ Jesus*	adverb clause
Through what means?	*in me*	prepositional phrase
Under what condition?	*in Christ Jesus*	prepositional phrase
Why?	*because of my coming to you again*	prepositional phrases
To whom?	*to you*	prepositional phrase
How often?	*again*	single word

As we have seen in previous chapters, <u>it is not important for Bible study that you be able to identify the particular structure of an adverb. The important thing is to recognize that a word or group of words is answering one of the adverb questions in the chart at the beginning of this chapter.</u> One does this by saying the verb and then asking the adverb questions.

Notice that the adverbs in the following verses teach us important aspects of the sinful life.

- *And you were dead in your trespasses and sins, in which you formerly walked according to the course of this world, according to the prince of the power of the air, of the spirit that is now working in the sons of disobedience.* (Ephesians 2:1-2, NASB).

"walked" **when?**	*formerly*
"you formerly walked" **how?**	*according to the course of this world*
"you formerly walked" **how?**	*according to the prince of the power of the air, of the spirit that is now working in the sons of disobedience*
"working" **when?**	*now*
"working" **where?**	*in the sons of disobedience*

God is light (1 John 1:5), and as the world continues to ignore his sovereignty and to reject his commands and decrees, earth becomes a darker place to live. However, Christians are like stars in that they radiate God and shine with his characteristics. The adverbs in this next passage clarify how we are to live in order to do this and why that is important.

- *Do everything without complaining or arguing, so that you may become blameless and pure, children of God without fault in a crooked and depraved generation, in which you shine like stars in the universe.* (Philippians 2:15, NIV).

"Do everything" **how?**	*without complaining or arguing*
"Do everything without complaining or arguing" **why?**	*so that you may become blameless and pure, children of God without fault in a crooked and depraved generation, in which you shine like stars in the universe*
"you shine" **how?**	*like stars in the universe*

"Without complaining and arguing" tells us how to we are to "do everything," and the next phrase clarifies why we are to do this. The final adverb phrase is a comparison, describing how we will shine if we do this. Paul is being both specific and unrelenting when he tells us how we should do everything. The challenge of these adverbs is hard to avoid.

The adverbs in the following passage, along with the adjectival structures (see Chapters 7 and 8), clarify the operation of God's power. These structures shed light on the simple sentence "to him [God] be glory."

- *Now to him who is able to do immeasurably more than all we ask or imagine, according to his power that is at work within us, to him be glory in the church and in Christ Jesus throughout all generations, for ever and ever! Amen.* (Ephesians 3:20-21, NIV).

When?	*now*
To whom?	*to him who is able to do more than all we ask or imagine*
"do" how?	*according to his power that is at work within us*
"is at work" where?	*within us*
"be glory" to whom?	*to him*
"be glory" where?	*in the church and in Christ Jesus*
"be glory" to what extent?	*throughout all generations*
"be glory" how long?	*for ever and ever*

The first adverb, "now," tells us that glory is due to the Lord at all times. The phrase "to him who is able to do more than all we ask or imagine" tells us to whom the glory is due at all times. "According to his power that is at work within us" is interesting because it tells us both how God is able and explains that God's power works within us, which would give us the ability to give him glory in the first place. Finally, through the adverbs we learn the recipient of this glory (God), the glory's extent, and its duration.

The adverbs in the next passage are key to understanding the meaning. They give details for how often we are to praise God, how and where we are to praise God, why we praise God, and, most importantly, how we praise God. Without the adverbs, these verses simply say, "Speak to each other" and "give thanks."

- *Speak to each other with psalms, hymns, and spiritual songs, singing and making music in your hearts to the Lord. Always give thanks to God the Father for everything, in the name of our Lord Jesus Christ.* (Ephesians 5: 19–20, NCV).

"speak to each other" how?	*with psalms, hymns, and spiritual songs*
"speak to each other" how?	*singing* *and* *making music in your hearts to the Lord*
"making music" where?	*in your hearts*
"making music" to whom?	*to the Lord*
"give thanks" how often?	*always*
"always give thanks" to whom?	*to God the Father*
"always give thanks" why?	*for everything*
"always give thanks to God the Father for everything" how?	*in the name of our Lord Jesus Christ*

If we did not have adverbs to focus our attention and our reason to give thanks, this command would be incredibly general. Instead, it is followed by adverbs that answer almost every question we could ask about singing and giving thanks.

Adverbs have no specific location in the sentence; they can be found nearly anywhere. However, if an adverb comes at the beginning of a sentence, that adverb has emphasis in the sentence.

- ***To the faithful,*** *you show yourself faithful,* ***to the blameless*** *you show yourself blameless,* ***to the pure*** *you show yourself pure, but* ***to the crooked*** *you show yourself shrewd.* (Psalm 18:25-26, NIV). The psalmist places emphasis upon the adverbial prepositional phrases "to the faithful," "to the blameless," "to the pure," and "to the crooked" by putting them first rather than at the end of the clause. This way, we understand to whom exactly the psalmist wants us to show ourselves in each case.

- *I will lead the blind by a way they do not know;* ***along unfamiliar paths*** *I will guide them.* (Isaiah 42:16, NIV). In this verse, Isaiah tells where God will guide his people: "along unfamiliar paths." The inverted structure of this verse catches the reader's attention because he may not be expecting God to guide his people along unfamiliar paths, and this prepositional phrase draws attention because it comes first.

- ***Without wood,*** *fire goes out;* ***without a gossip,*** *conflict dies down.* (Proverbs 26:20, HCSB). Here, the conditions are put before the actual point of the sentence. "Fire goes out" under what condition? "Without wood." "Conflict dies down" under what condition? "Without gossip."

Because these verses do not follow the usual pattern, in which adverbs are located close to the verb, the adverbs are emphasized.

Significance of Adverbs in Bible Sentences

Knowledge of adverbs can be an important tool when interpreting the Bible for a number of reasons. It is always worth looking for answers to the adverb questions in a passage of Scripture. What follows are a few of the reasons for doing so.

To Understand the Details of the Narrative

- *The LORD has broken the rod of the wicked, the scepter of rulers, which* ***in anger*** *struck down peoples* ***with unceasing blows,*** *and* ***in fury*** *subdued nations* ***with relentless aggression.*** (Isaiah 14:5-6, NIV). Each action is modified with an adverb clause of manner ("in anger," "in fury") and one of instrument ("with unceasing blows," "with relentless aggression").

- *Many followed him and he healed all their sick,* ***warning them not to tell who he was.*** (Matthew 12:15-16, NIV). This adds to the narrative in that it tells under what condition Christ healed the sick. The condition under which Christ healed the sick was that they did not tell who he was. This adverbial phrase, starting with "warning," gives extra insight into Jesus' character. The main part of the sentence shows us that Jesus had power over sickness and that he was compassionate. The adverbial phrase at the end shows that Jesus did not want the people to spread news of him because of his ability to heal. He was not looking for that kind of fame at that point in his ministry.

- *And* ***taking the five loaves and the two fish*** *he looked up to heaven and said a blessing and broke the loaves and gave them* ***to the disciples to set before the people***. *And he divided the two fish* ***among them all***. (Mark 6:41, ESV). The adverbial phrase that begins the sentence explains under what conditions Jesus thanked God and began to feed the people. As Jesus received a blessing from God, he gave thanks to God and fixed his focus heavenward. The second sentence has the three adverbial phrases ("to his disciples," "to set before the people," and "before the people"). Respectively, the phrases answer to whom, why, and where he gave the loaves. The second sentence includes "among them all," telling us how they were divided.

- *The natives showed us extraordinary kindness; for **because of the rain that had set in** and **because of the cold**, they kindled a fire and received us all. But **when Paul had gathered a bundle of sticks and laid them on the fire**, a viper came out **because of the heat** and fastened itself **on his hand**.* (Acts 28:2-3, NASB). Without adverbs, this narrative would lose much of its most important detail. We wouldn't know why Paul and his companions were welcomed or why the islanders built a fire. We wouldn't know that Paul looked for kindling, why the viper came out of hiding, and where it fastened itself. It would be possible to tell this story without adverbs, but the narrative would be choppy and awkward.

- *Coming to his hometown, he began teaching the people **in their synagogue**, and they were amazed.* (Matthew 13:54, NIV). The adverb in this sentence tells where Jesus was teaching, which has implications both in itself and in that it helps explain many events that occur later.

To Understand Metaphors or Abstract Concepts

Sometimes the adverbs help us to understand that a metaphor is being used, or the adverb can help us to understand an abstract concept within the context.

- *I am weary from my crying; my throat is parched. My eyes fail, **looking for my God**.* (Psalm 69:3, HCSB). Why is the writer worn out? Why do his eyes fail? The adverb shows that it is a metaphoric failing of the eyes rather than a literal one. Without those adverbs that tell under what conditions the writer is worn and blind, there would be no reason not to take the writer literally. Rather, the point in this verse is that the writer is desperate, not that the writer is physically weak or is going blind.

- *Have this attitude **in yourselves** which was also **in Christ Jesus**, who, although He existed **in the form of God**, did not regard equality with God a thing to be grasped, but emptied Himself, **taking the form of a bond-servant**, and **being made in the likeness of men**.* (Philippians 2:5-7, NASB). Adverbs answer not only where this attitude was first manifested and where it should be now, but tell of Christ's existence with God, and how Christ made himself into nothing, a concept that would be difficult for us to understand without the adverbs. In this verse, Christ made himself nothing by "taking the form of a bond-servant" and by "being made in the likeness of man." Notice the passive verb "being made," which implies a doer of the action (see Chapter 4).

- *"**In returning and rest** you shall be saved; **in quietness and confidence** shall be your strength."* (Isaiah 30:15b, NKJV). God is telling the people of Israel through what means they could find their salvation and their strength and saying that they are rejecting the very means to their salvation and strength. The adverbs here are important for the people of Israel to understand what they must do so that they can gain these benefits.

To Give Context for the Application

Another major way that adverbs are important for Bible study is that they provide important context for application. Key adverb questions here are "why?" "how?" and "under what conditions?"

For example, in Matthew 6:14-15, the adverb phrases tell us the conditions under which we are or are not forgiven. The adverbs are vital in this passage. Without the context they provide, we would miss some important instruction.

- ***If you forgive men when they sin against you**, your heavenly Father will also forgive you. But **if you do not forgive men their sins**, your Father will not forgive your sins. (Matthew 6:14-15, NIV).*

Action	Adverb Question	Answer
you forgive men	When?	*when they sin against you*
they sin	Toward whom?	*against you*
your Heavenly Father will also forgive you	Under what conditions?	*if you forgive men when they sin against you*
your Father will not forgive your sins	Under what conditions?	*if you do not forgive men their sins*

The adverbs here provide important information to clarify when we are or are not forgiven. It clarifies that when we forgive those who sin against us, we will be forgiven. This specifies when we are to forgive others: when they have sinned against us. This is further specified when the question "to whom" is answered; we are to forgive others when they sin against us. We are then told that the heavenly Father will forgive us, but the adverb phrase at the beginning clarifies the conditions under which God will forgive us: "If you forgive men when they sin against you." Then the passage says that God will sometimes not forgive your sins, but the conditions are given as well: "if you do not forgive men their sins." The adverbs here are vital for understanding the context of the passage.

Romans 10:9 uses adverbs to tell us what we must do to be saved. Therefore, in this verse, the adverbs give the context for the application.

- ***If you confess with your mouth that Jesus is Lord and believe in your heart that God raised him from the dead**, you will be saved. (Romans 10:9, NLT).*

Action	Adverb Question	Answer
you confess	How?	*with your mouth*
believe… that God raised Him from the dead	How? / Where?	*in your heart*
God raised him	Under what conditions?	*from the dead*
you will be saved	Under what conditions?	*if you confess with your mouth "Jesus is Lord"* *and* (if you) *believe in your heart that God raised Him from the dead*

That two-part adverb of condition is vital. These two adverbs give us the context for salvation, the central concept of the gospel. Under what conditions will I be saved? "If [I] confess with [my] mouth, "Jesus is Lord," and believe in [my] heart that God raised him from the dead, [I] will be saved."

The adverbs in the next example again give the context for a possible application of the verse.

- *Jotham became powerful, **because he always obeyed the LORD his God**. (2 Chronicles 27:6, NCV).*

Action	Adverb Question	Answer
became powerful	Why?	*because he always obeyed the LORD his God*
he obeyed	How often?	*always*

We find out from the adverb phrases that it is because he walked steadfastly before the Lord that Jotham grew powerful.

The next passage has several actions that are clarified through adverbs. We are told how to trust in the Lord, where we should not trust, and when we should acknowledge him. It is through all of these adverbs that we gain the understanding that we should trust all the time completely in him and not at all in ourselves.

- *Trust in the LORD **with all your heart** and lean not **on your own understanding**; **in all your ways** acknowledge him, and he will make your paths straight.* (Proverbs 3:5-6, NIV).

Action	Adverb Question	Answer
trust in the lord	How?	*with all your heart*
lean not	Where?	*on your own understanding*
acknowledge him	When?	*in all your ways*

The adverbs in the Matthew passage that follows are important to the context of the passage. They tell under what conditions you should leave your gift at the altar and not continue worshipping until you have reconciled with your brother.

- *Therefore **if you bring your gift to the altar, and there remember that your brother has something against you**, leave your gift **there before the altar**, and go your way. **First** be reconciled **to your brother**, and **then** come and offer your gift.* (Matthew 5:23-24, NKJV).

Action	Adverb Question	Answer
leave your gift there before the altar	Under what condition?	*if* *you bring your gift to the altar* *and* *there remember that your brother has something against you*
leave your gift	Where?	*before the altar*
leave your gift	Where?	*there*
be reconciled	In what order?	*first*
be reconciled	To whom?	*to your brother*
come and offer your gift	In what order?	*then*

The basic sentence below is a picture of a man with worthless religion. Under what condition is it worthless? The bolded adverbial clause explains the condition of the man's mind, actions, and heart that all work together to nullify his religion.

- ***If anyone thinks himself to be religious and yet does not bridle his tongue but deceives his own heart**, this man's religion is worthless.* (James 1: 26, NASB).

Action	Adverb Question	Answer
this man's religion is worthless	Under what conditions?	*if* *anyone thinks himself to be religious* *and yet* *does not bridle his tongue* *but* *deceives his own heart*

Most people do not naturally rejoice in suffering. This next verse, however, gives us the command to do exactly that.

- *Consider it a great joy, my brothers, **whenever you experience various trials**, **knowing that the testing of your faith produces endurance**.* (James 1:2-3, HCSB).

Action	Adverb Question	Answer
consider it a great joy, my brothers	Under what conditions?	*whenever you experience various trials*
consider it a great joy, my brothers, whenever you experience various trials	Why?	*knowing that the testing of your faith produces endurance*

Instead of forcing us to obey without knowing *why*, the passage goes on to explain the purpose of suffering. We don't rejoice because we suffer; we rejoice because of the result of suffering: perseverance.

Packed with adverbs, this next verse first tells us how we ought to obey our earthly masters—respectfully, fearfully, and sincerely. It also tells us when we should obey them and calls us to integrity by answering the "why" adverb question, saying that we should not work for the purpose of pleasing men, but with the intent of pleasing Christ.

- *Slaves, obey your earthly masters **with respect and fear**, and **with sincerity of heart**, **just as you would obey Christ**. Obey them **not only to win their favor when their eye is on you**, but **like slaves of Christ, doing the will of God from your heart**.* (Ephesians 6:5-6, NIV).

Action	Adverb Question	Answer
slaves, obey your earthly masters	How?	*with respect* *and* *[with] fear,* *and* *with sincerity of heart,* *just as you would obey Christ*
obey them	Under what conditions?	*not only to win their favor when their eye is on you*

Action	Adverb Question	Answer
obey them	Compared to what?	*like slaves of Christ*
obey them	How?	*doing the will of God from your heart*
doing the will of God	How?	*from your heart*

The last example in this section is inverted (see Chapter 3). The adverb is important because it tells the reason that the man who perseveres under trial is blessed. It also tells us when he will receive his blessing—after he has persevered.

- *Blessed is the man who endures temptation;* **for when he has been approved, he will receive the crown of life which the Lord has promised to those who love Him**. (James 1:12, NKJV).

Action	Adverb Question	Answer
blessed is the man who endures temptation	Why?	*for when he has been approved, he will receive the crown of life which the lord has promised to those who love him*
he will receive the crown of life which the lord has promised to those who love him	When?	*when he has been approved*

To Reveal Important Theological Truths

Finally, we rely upon adverbs in some cases to give us important theological truths.

- **For in the gospel** *a righteousness from God is revealed, a righteousness that is* **by faith from first to last,** *just as it is written: "The righteous will live* **by faith.**" (Romans 1:17, NIV). This verse contains several adverb phrases modifying different verbs. In the first phrase, the adverb tells us where the righteousness from God is revealed: "in the gospel." The second phrase tells us that this righteousness exists. By what means? And for how long? Righteousness is "by faith" and "from first to last." Finally, the adverb in the last line tells us by what means or how the righteous should live: "the righteous shall live by faith." The adverbs in Romans 1:17 describe the doctrine of salvation and righteousness by faith and also sum up the Christian life.

- *But you, O Bethlehem Ephrathah, are only a small village among all the people of Judah. Yet a ruler of Israel will come* **from you,** *one whose origins are* **from the distant past.** (Micah 5:2, NLT). Two important truths about the origin of Christ come from the adverb phrases. First, Christ will come from Bethlehem. Perhaps more importantly, Christ is "from the distant past." Christ existed before time.

- *For* **by him** *all things were created: things* **in heaven** *and* **on earth,** *visible and invisible, whether thrones or powers or rulers or authorities; all things were created* **by him** *and* **for him.** *He is* **before all things,** *and* **in him** *all things hold together.* (Colossians 1:16-17, NIV). In this passage, there are several adverbial prepositional phrases that convey theological truths about the nature of Christ. In verse 16, we learn Christ's role in creation: he is both an agent ("by him") and the reason ("for him") for creation. In verse 17, the adverb phrase "in him" modifies the verb "hold together": Christ is the location in which everything holds together.

- ***If we say that we have fellowship with Him and yet walk in the darkness***, *we lie and do not practice the truth; but **if we walk in the Light as He Himself is in the Light**, we have fellowship with one another, and the blood of Jesus His Son cleanses us **from all sin**. **If we say that we have no sin**, we are deceiving ourselves and the truth is not **in us**. **If we confess our sins**, He is faithful and righteous to forgive us our sins and to cleanse us **from all unrighteousness**. **If we say that we have not sinned**, we make Him a liar and His word is not **in us**.* (1 John1: 6-10, NASB).

The many adverbs in this passage add a great deal to our understanding. In this passage, there are five adverbial clauses that start with the word "if." In this case, they all are acting as questions of condition, telling the reader the surrounding conditions of the statement. For example, we lie and do not practice the truth under what conditions? If we say that we have fellowship with him and yet walk in the darkness. Adverbs also tell us to what extent we are cleansed: from *all* sin and from *all* unrighteousness. We are also given adverbs that represent a place that is a metaphor: "in the darkness" and "in the Light." These adverbs are in a contrasting parallel. An adverb of manner tells us how we are supposed to walk: "as He Himself is in the light." Another adverb of place ("in us") is used twice to tell us where the truth and his word need to be.

Sometimes we can learn theological truths because no adverbs are present. For example, the lack of adverbs can signify an unconditional statement. These can be found particularly in references to God's character or actions. Notice that the lack of adverbs in the verses below shows an unconditional statement.

- *God is love.* (1 John 4:16, NKJV).
- *God is light.* (1 John 1:5, NCV).
- *The Lord is my light and my salvation.* (Psalm 27:1, ESV).
- *The Lord reigns!* (Psalm 97:1; 99:1, NIV).

Questions for Analyzing Adverbs

In summary, when trying to understand the significance of adverbial structures in Scripture, ask and answer these questions:

1. Find words or groups of words that answer adverb questions.
    - Which questions do they answer? What are the adverbs telling us?
2. What is the purpose for the adverb? Does it do any of the following?
    - Help us understand the details of the narrative
    - Help us understand metaphors or abstract concepts
    - Give important context for the application of the verse
    - Reveal important theological truths

Some Practice

Matthew 14:13

- *Hearing of this, the crowds followed Him on foot from the towns.* (NIV).

The referent for "this" is referring to the death of John the Baptist. When Christ withdrew to be alone, the crowds followed him. "Hearing of this" is therefore an adverbial phrase of reason. There are other adverbs in this passage as well: "on foot" is an adverb of manner, and "from the towns" is an adverb of origin. All of these adverbs help to clarify the details of the narrative.

Matthew 13:3b – 9

- *A sower went out to sow. And as he sowed, some seeds fell along the path, and the birds came and devoured them. Other seeds fell on rocky ground, where they did not have much soil, and immediately they sprang up, since they had no depth of soil, but when the sun rose they were scorched. And since they had no root, they withered away. Other seeds fell among thorns, and the thorns grew up and choked them. Other seeds fell on good soil and produced grain, some a hundredfold, some sixty, some thirty. He who has ears, let him hear. (ESV).*

The adverbs of destination (where the seeds fell in each case) are emphasized in this parable since the author wants the reader to notice where the seeds are falling. The destination of the seeds determines the result. The adverbs are important to understanding the application of the parable.

Romans 5:1

- *Therefore, since we have been justified by faith, we have peace with God through our Lord Jesus Christ. (ESV).*

This passage uses adverbs to convey important theological truths. The sentence without adverbs is simply, "We have peace." "Since we have been justified by faith" is an adverb clause of reason, including within it an adverb prepositional phrase of agency; justification comes "by faith." The phrase "through our Lord Jesus Christ" is an adverbial phrase of means. Christ is the means through which we can have peace with God.

Luke 4:31-32

- *Then He went down to Capernaum, a town in Galilee, and was teaching them on the Sabbath. They were astonished at His teaching because His message had authority. (HCSB).*

This is an example of adverbs clarifying the details of the narrative. There are three minor adverbs: "to Capernaum" is Jesus' destination, "on the Sabbath" tells when he was teaching, and "at his teaching" describes why the crowds were astonished. However, the most significant is "because his message had authority," which tells why the crowds were astonished at his teaching.

Colossians 1:18

- *He is also head of the body, the church; and He is the beginning, the firstborn from the dead, so that He Himself will come to have first place in everything. (NASB).*

In this passage, the adverb clarifies an abstract concept or metaphor. Paul calls Christ the "head of the body" and "the firstborn," which are both metaphorical in nature. The adverb phrase of result clarifies the use of these metaphors: "so that he himself will come to have first place in everything." Paul describes Christ in these ways, and then shows the implications and result of Christ's nature.

1 Corinthians 1:10

- *I appeal to you, brothers, in the name of our Lord Jesus Christ, that all of you agree with one another so that there may be no divisions among you and that you may be perfectly united in mind and thought. (NIV).*

The adverbs in this passage help provide context for the application. Paul tells the Corinthians and us that the goal is for Christians to not merely be united but to be "perfectly" united. Furthermore, it tells us how we are to be united: "in mind and thought." The passage also tells the reason for everyone agreeing with one another: "so that there may be no divisions among you." These adverbs help clarify how the idea of unity can be applied in our lives.

1 Peter 1:3-5

- *Blessed be the God and Father of our Lord Jesus Christ, who according to His great mercy has caused us to be born again to a living hope through the resurrection of Jesus Christ from the dead, to obtain an inheritance which is imperishable and undefiled and will not fade away, reserved in heaven for you, who are protected by the power of God through faith for a salvation ready to be revealed in the last time.* (NASB).

This passage uses adverbs to reveal important theological truths.

Question	Adverb Phrase	Commentary
Why?	*according to His great mercy*	God caused us to be born again because his mercy toward us is great.
How often?	*again*	This is our second birth.
Where? To what?	*to a living hope*	Our rebirth has now brought us to a metaphorical place of fresh perspective in Christ, a state of being, not static but living
By what means?	*through the resurrection of Jesus Christ from the dead*	The extended phrase functions as the means by which we are reborn to a living hope: through Christ's rebirth from the dead.
Why?	*to obtain an inheritance*	We were born again for this reason.
Where?	*in heaven*	This is where the inheritance is reserved.
For whom?	*for you who are protected by the power of God*	This inheritance is for us.
How? By what means?	*by the power of God*	It emphasizes the instrumentality of his power as the means of our salvation
By what means?	*through faith*	The power of God works through faith.
Why?	*for a salvation ready to be revealed in the last time*	This shows the reason that God protects us.
When?	*in the last time*	This says when salvation will be revealed.

Chapter 10
Putting It All Together

One practical way to apply what we have discussed in this book is to conduct a full grammatical analysis of a particular passage of Scripture.

Phrase Analysis of Specific Passages

Psalm 15

The first passage is a poem from Psalms. In this psalm we have a detailed description of the actions of a righteous person, followed by a promise extended to that person (that he will never be shaken).

LORD, who may dwell in your sanctuary? Who may live on your holy hill? He whose walk is blameless and who does what is righteous, who speaks the truth from his heart and has no slander on his tongue, who does his neighbor no wrong and casts no slur on his fellowman, who despises a vile man but honors those who fear the LORD, who keeps his oath even when it hurts, who lends his money without usury and does not accept a bribe against the innocent. He who does these things will never be shaken. (NIV).

Sentences 1 and 2: *LORD, who may dwell in your sanctuary? Who may live on your holy hill?*

Word or Phrase	Type of Structure	Notes	Chapter with Concept
Lord	Noun of direct address	The Lord is the one of whom the question is being asked.	6
who may dwell	Basic subject and predicate Intransitive verb	When "who" is a part of a question, it stands in as the subject of the sentence. The action stops with the dwelling; anything that follows simply describes the circumstances surrounding the action.	2
In your sanctuary	Adverb of place Possessive pronoun "your"	This phrase tells us where the dwelling will be. The possessive pronoun "your" tells us whose place it is (the Lord's).	9 5
?	Question	This is a "regular" question, rather than a rhetorical one, so we will need to determine the answer (which comes up later in the passage).	3
who may live	Basic subject and predicate Intransitive verb	The "who" of this question is the same subject as in the previous sentence. The subject and predicate are an echo of "who may dwell." This is parallelism.	2 3
on your holy hill	Adverb of place Adjective "holy" Possessive pronoun "your"	Like the previous sentence, this clarifies the location of the dwelling, on the Lord's "holy hill." The adjective associates the hill with God. The place in the question seems to be metaphorical rather than an actual, physical place, since nowhere else in the Bible are we directed to God's holy hill.	9 7

Word or Phrase	Type of Structure	Notes	Chapter with Concept
?	Question	These two questions are parallel in form and content. This parallelism is a poetic device that gives emphasis to the question.	3

Sentence 3: *He whose walk is blameless and who does what is righteous, who speaks the truth from his heart and has no slander on his tongue, who does his neighbor no wrong and casts no slur on his fellowman, who despises a vile man but honors those who fear the LORD, who keeps his oath even when it hurts, who lends his money without usury and does not accept a bribe against the innocent.*

Word or Phrase	Type of Structure	Notes	Chapter with Concept
he	Subject Personal pronoun	The personal pronoun "he" refers to someone who is able to dwell with God, as mentioned in the two questions that come before. This pronoun and the others in this passage are masculine, but the NIV is following the convention that uses masculine pronouns for the singular form of a pronoun that can refer to either a male or female. This psalm does not seem to be restricting the meaning to males alone.	2 5 6
whose walk	Restrictive relative clause	The head is "he." It is important that this relative clause is restrictive because we need the relative clause to define who can dwell with God.	7 8
is blameless	Linking verb with predicate adjective	This predicate adjective describes one attribute of the walk of the man.	
and	Coordinating conjunction	"And" here shows a connection between these two relative clauses. It tells us that both of these elements are equal descriptions and closely related.	6
who does	Restrictive relative clause	This restrictive relative clause restates the meaning of the first one. This parallelism is a poetic device.	7 8 5
what	Pronoun	The pronoun "what" stands for a noun such as "activity."	
is	Linking verb		
righteous	Predicate adjective	The predicate adjective describes the activity ("what").	
who speaks the truth	Relative clause	This is the first of a set of relative clauses, all of which still have "he" as the head. This and the relative clauses that follow it define for us what it means to do what is righteous.	7 8 9 3
from his heart	Adverb of origin	The truth comes from his heart.	
and	Coordinating conjunction	Notice again that this coordinating conjunction joins two verb phrases that say very similar things in a similar format. This is parallelism.	
has no slander			
on his tongue	Adverb of place	The adverb of place is a poetic way of saying that the man does not slander.	

Word or Phrase	Type of Structure	Notes	Chapter with Concept
who does his neighbor no wrong	Relative clause	The first verb phrase in this relative clause has an indirect object followed by a direct object. He does what? (no wrong) To whom? (his neighbor).	
and	Coordinating conjunction	Notice again the parallelism (with the coordinating conjunction joining two verb phrases that say very similar things in a similar format.)	2 8 6 3 9
casts no slur			
on his fellowman	Adverb of destination	The adverb of destination is a poetic way of saying where the slur would go.	
who despises a vile man	Relative clause	This relative clause also belongs to the head "he."	
but	Coordinating conjunction	"But" in this relative clause indicates an equal yet opposite relationship. The verb "despises" is opposite to "honors." Also, "a vile man" is opposite to "those who fear the Lord." The conjunction creates a contrasting parallelism.	7 8 6 3 5
honors those who fear the lord	Relative clause attached to the demonstrative pronoun head "those"	This verb phrase has another relative clause within it. This restrictive relative clause restricts the meaning of "those" to people who fear the Lord. Note the demonstrative pronoun. A definite pronoun such as "these" would change the meaning and would have excluded people living now.	
who keeps his oath	Relative clause	See earlier notes about the relative clauses.	
even when it hurts	Adverb of condition	The adverb phrase in this relative clause tells us the conditions under which the man keeps his oath—even when it hurts.	8 9
who lends his money	Relative clause	See earlier notes about the relative clauses.	
without usury	Adverb of manner	How does his lend his money? Without usury.	
and	Coordinating conjunction	The "and" links two equal, related ideas. Both of these have to do with money.	8 9 6 7
does not accept a bribe against the innocent	Adjectival prepositional phrase	The phrase "against the innocent" describes the type of bribe.	
[may dwell in God's sanctuary or live on his holy hill]	Ellipsis (words left out)	Notice that so far in the third sentence, we have only a much-extended subject. The subject is "he" with a series of relative clauses attached. Therefore, this is not a complete sentence. It is an answer to the first two questions, but it does not contain a main verb to go along with the subject. That has been left out.	3

Sentence 4: *He who does these things will never be shaken.*

Word or Phrase	Type of Structure	Notes	Chapter with Concept
he	Subject Personal pronoun	"He" is the subject, as defined by the restrictive relative clause that follows.	
who does	Restrictive relative clause	Since this clause is not set off by commas, we know that it is restrictive. This is important because the subject is restricted to only those who have the qualifications listed in the previous sentence.	8 5 6
these things	Demonstrative determiner "these"	The demonstrative determiner "these" points back to the list of relative clauses above.	
will never be shaken	Passive verb	This passive does not have a "by-phrase" to tell us what or who the original doer of the action is. The passive indicates that it is possible for someone or something outside of the person to shake him. However, since the "*by*-phrase" is not included and context does not give us a clue, we can conclude that this doer is not important since the subject will never be shaken.	4 9
never	Adverb of frequency	The adverb tells us that this will not happen. No one or any outside circumstances can shake this righteous person.	

James 1: 26-27

The next example is a piece of instruction. Two very different "religions" are portrayed. Notice especially the use of adjectives to describe, verb phrases to show actions, and noun appositives to define.

If anyone thinks himself to be religious, and yet does not bridle his tongue but deceives his own heart, this man's religion is worthless. This is pure and undefiled religion in the sight of our God and Father, to visit orphans and widows in their distress, and to keep oneself unstained by the world. (NASB).

Sentence 1: *If anyone thinks himself to be religious, and yet does not bridle his tongue but deceives his own heart, this man's religion is worthless.*

Word or Phrase	Type of Structure	Notes	Chapter with Concept
if anyone thinks himself to be religious, and yet does not bridle his tongue but deceives his own heart	Adverb of condition	"If" is a subordinating conjunction that suggests a possibility. It introduces an adverb of condition. In this case, the condition is a person thinking that he is religious and not bridling his tongue and therefore deceiving himself. This adverb sets the stage for the main clause.	6 9

Word or Phrase	Type of Structure	Notes	Chapter with Concept
to be religious	Adjective	"To be religious" is an adjective describing "himself." Notice that James is saying that the person thinks that he *is* religious, a main characteristic of his nature: to **be** religious rather than to **act** in a religious manner. This makes his self-deception even more extreme. He does not merely think that he does religious acts but that he is religious.	2 7
and yet	Coordinating conjunction	Using both these two coordinators shows that the verb phrase that follows is equal and yet contrasting with the first verb phrase. "Yet" as a conjunction shows a contrast.	6 2
does not bridle his tongue	Transitive negative verb with direct object	"His tongue" is the direct object of "bridle."	
but	Coordinating conjunction	Here is another contrast signaled by the conjunction "but." This verb phrase "deceives his own heart" provides another contrast with thinking oneself to be religious.	6 2 3
deceives his own heart	Transitive verb with direct object	"His own heart" is the direct object of "deceives." The verb is transitive. One must deceive someone or something. Notice that these last two verb phrases are the same structure (with a transitive verb and direct object), forming a type of parallelism that highlights a contrast.	
this man's religion is worthless	Basic subject and predicate	This is the basic subject and predicate. What preceded it was all an adverb of condition. This man's religion is worthless under what conditions? (Under the conditions just stated.)	2 5 7
	Demonstrative determiner "this"	"This" refers to the "anyone" at the beginning of the sentence.	
	Predicate adjective "worthless"	The predicate adjective "worthless" describes one characteristic of the religion of a person who is careless with his words and practices self-deception. It is a strong adjective worth pondering.	

Sentence 2: *This is pure and undefiled religion in the sight of our God and Father, to visit orphans and widows in their distress, and to keep oneself unstained by the world.*

Word or Phrase	Type of Structure	Notes	Chapter With Concept
this is pure and undefiled religion	Basic subject and predicate		2
this	Demonstrative pronoun "this"	The pronoun "this" must have a referent somewhere in the context. In this case, the referent comes in the two noun appositives that follow.	
is pure and undefiled religion	Linking verb with predicate nominative	The predicate nominative ("pure and undefiled religion") gives one definition of the subject ("this").	6 5 7
pure and undefiled	Two adjectives joined by coordinating conjunction	Think about what these two similar adjectives are saying about religion. Again, they are strong adjectives contrasting with "worthless."	
in the sight of our God and Father	Adjectival modifier attached to head "pure and undefiled religion"	Another adjective structure is attached to "pure and undefiled religion." It adds to the meaning of this religion.	
to visit orphans and widows	Noun appositive	A noun appositive renames or defines its head. In this case, the head is "pure and undefiled religion in the sight of our God and Father."	5 9
in their distress	Adverb of time	The adverb of time tells when orphans and widows are to be visited.	
and	Coordinating conjunction	The coordinating conjunction links two equal and related ideas. It is important to note the use of these two noun appositives linked as equal and related. The first one is an outward act and the second one is an inward purity. Both of these constitute pure and undefiled religion in the sight of God.	6
to keep oneself unstained by the world	Noun appositive	This is a second noun appositive defining the head "pure and undefiled religion in the sight of our God and Father."	5 7
unstained by the world	Completed adjective	Note that the completed adjective is "unstained by the world," not merely unstained. We need the entire adjective phrase for a complete meaning.	

Ephesians 3:14 – 19

For this reason I bow my knees before the Father, from whom every family in heaven and on earth is named, that according to the riches of his glory he may grant you to be strengthened with power through his Spirit in your inner being, so that Christ may dwell in your hearts through faith—that you, being rooted and grounded in love, may have strength to comprehend with all the saints what is the breadth and length and height and depth, and to know the love of Christ that surpasses knowledge, that you may be filled with all the fullness of God. (ESV).

Word or Phrase	Type of Structure	Notes	Chapter With Concept
for this reason	Adverb of reason Demonstrative determiner "this"	The determiner "this" must have a referent. It is possible that Paul is referencing the material that precedes this sentence since he has been speaking about his ministry. He has just said that his sufferings are the glory of the Ephesians. However, since four reasons are given in this sentence, it is more likely that the "this" refers to the four reasons that follow.	9 6
I bow my knees *before the Father*	Basic subject and predicate Adverb of place/condition	This is the basic part of this long sentence. Paul is using a metaphor (bowing one's knees before God) to indicate his ministry.	2 9
from whom *every family* *in heaven and on earth* *is named*	Entire clause is a nonrestrictive relative clause attached to the head "the Father" Determiner "every" Adjective attachment Passive verb, not active	Nonrestrictive relative clauses are set off by punctuation and merely add additional description to the noun head. This relative clause tells us more about the father. "Every" is a quantifier; it includes all. The adjectival attachment "in heaven and on earth" further describes "every family." Every family in heaven and earth is named from God.	8 5 7 4
that *according to the riches of his glory* *he* *may grant* *[for] you to be strengthened* *you* *with power* *through his Spirit* *In your inner being*	Entire clause is an adverb of reason Adverb of extent Personal pronoun Transitive verb with direct object Personal pronoun Adverb of manner Adverb of means Adverb of place	**Reason number 1 for why Paul bows his knee to God** "According to the riches of his glory" is to a huge extent. "He" refers to the Father. A transitive verb has a direct object. He may grant what? *[for] you to be strengthened.* "You" are the saints in Ephesus. How? *With power* Through what means? *Through his Spirit* Where? *In your inner being*	9 6 2

Word or Phrase	Type of Structure	Notes	Chapter With Concept
so that	Entire clause is an adverb of reason	**Reason number 2 for why Paul bows his knee to God**	
Christ may dwell	Basic subject and predicate of this clause	*Christ may dwell*	9 2
in your hearts	Adverb of place	Where? *In your hearts*	
through faith	Adverb of means	Through what means? *Through faith*	
that	Entire clause is an adverb of reason	**Reason number 3 for why Paul bows his knee to God**	
you, being rooted [in love] and grounded in love,	Pronoun head "you" with adjectival participial phrase (with ellipsis)	"You" are the saints in Ephesus. They are rooted in love as well as being grounded in love. This adjectival description is important because their "grounding" in love is foundational to having strength.	9 6 3 7
may have strength to comprehend… and to know….	Adjectival infinitive phrases describing the head "strength"	The adjectival attachments are vital. It is not merely strength, but strength to comprehend something and to know something (see next sections).	
[*strength*] *to comprehend*	Adjectival infinitive phrase	It is not mere strength; it is strength to comprehend something.	
with all the saints	Adverb of association	Comprehend with whom? *All the saints*	7 9 2
what is the breadth and length and height and depth	Direct object of "comprehend"	A transitive verb must have a direct object. This tells what they are to comprehend.	
and	Coordinating conjunction	An "and" joins related and equal ideas.	6
[*strength*] *to know*	Adjectival infinitive phrase	It is not mere strength; it is strength to know something.	
the love of Christ	Direct object of "know"	A transitive verb must have a direct object. This tells what they are to know: *the love of Christ.*	7 2 8
that surpasses knowledge	Relative clause that describes the head "the love of Christ"	Relative clauses are adjectival and give us more description of the head. This is not ordinary love.	
that	Entire clause is an adverb of reason	**Reason number 4 for why Paul bows his knee to God**	
you	Personal pronoun	"You" are the saints in Ephesus.	9 6 4
may be filled	Passive verb	The passive verb means that the subject is not the doer of the action. This is a divine passive. God is doing the filling. We can't do it for ourselves.	
with all the fullness of God	Adverb of manner	How will they be filled? *With all the fullness of God*	

Reread this entire sentence again and, as you do so, find the four reasons Paul gives for his ministry. Notice especially the meaning that is added by the adverbs, the adjectival infinitive phrases, and the divine passive verb.

Romans 10:9-15

The next passage is from Romans and gives us doctrinal explanation.

That if you confess with your mouth, "Jesus is Lord," and believe in your heart that God raised him from the dead, you will be saved. For it is with your heart that you believe and are justified, and it is with your mouth that you confess and are saved. As the Scripture says, "Anyone who trusts in him will never be put to shame." For there is no difference between Jew and Gentile—the same Lord is Lord of all and richly blesses all who call on him, for, "Everyone who calls on the name of the Lord will be saved." How, then, can they call on the one they have not believed in? And how can they believe in the one of whom they have not heard? And how can they hear without someone preaching to them? And how can they preach unless they are sent? As it is written, "How beautiful are the feet of those who bring good news!" (NIV).

Sentence 1: *That if you confess with your mouth, "Jesus is Lord," and believe in your heart that God raised him from the dead, you will be saved.*

Word or Phrase	Type of Structure	Notes	Chapter with Concept
that ….	Start of a noun appositive	The word "that" at the beginning of a clause makes it into a noun clause, not an independent clause. Therefore, this entire sentence is acting as a noun appositive renaming a noun head. The noun head comes directly before the appositive. In this case, we need to look to the previous verse to get the noun head "the word of faith we are proclaiming." Therefore, as an appositive, this entire sentence defines the word of faith. This is an example of a situation in which the previous verse provides important information.	5
if	Subordinating conjunction	"If" shows that this clause is an adverb of condition.	5 6 2 9
you	Personal pronoun	At the beginning of this chapter, Paul uses the noun of direct address "brothers." We assume that this is the specific referent for the pronoun, but we can extend it to all Christians.	
confess	Transitive verb	The transitive verb has a direct object coming up.	
with your mouth	Adverb of manner	The adverb answers how we should confess.	
"Jesus is Lord"	Direct object of the transitive verb	The transitive verb "confess" has a direct object, something specific that we need to confess: the statement that Jesus is Lord.	

Word or Phrase	Type of Structure	Notes	Chapter with Concept
and	Coordinating conjunction	This conjunction signals that something just as important as what came before it will come next. This is an addition. (Think about the implication if "or" had been used instead of "and.") Notice that both of these verb phrases joined by "and" are in the same pattern: a transitive verb, adverb of manner, and direct object of the transitive verb. Therefore, this verse shows parallelism.	6 2 3
believe *in your heart* *that God raised him* *from the dead*	Transitive verb Adverb of manner Direct object of the transitive verb Adverb of condition	The transitive verb has a direct object coming up. *Believe* how? *In your heart* As the direct object, it shows us what we need to believe. *Believe* what? *That God raised him from the dead.* God raised him from what condition? *From the dead.*	2 9
you will be saved *will be saved*	Basic subject and predicate Passive conditional verb phrase	The verb is very important here. The passive implies that someone else is doing the saving. In this case, it is a divine passive: God is saving us; we can't save ourselves. Also, the word "will" makes the verb conditional. This sentence started with an "if" clause. If we fulfill the ideas in that clause, we will be saved.	5 2 4

Sentence 2: *For it is with your heart that you believe and are justified, and it is with your mouth that you confess and are saved.*

Word or Phrase	Type of Structure	Notes	Chapter with Concept
for	Conjunction	The "for" signals that this sentence is giving the explanation for the sentence before it. These two sentences could have been one sentence because in Edited American English we don't start a sentence with a coordinating conjunction.	6
it is with your heart that you believe and are justified	Extraposed sentence	This extraposed sentence could be rewritten as "you believe with your heart and are justified." Having it extraposed gives emphasis to the adverb of instrument "with your heart." This concept is important enough for the emphasis. (See next section)	3
it is	Placeholder subject	The "it" is just a placeholder. The logical subject comes after the verb in an extraposed sentence.	

Word or Phrase	Type of Structure	Notes	Chapter with Concept
with your heart	Adverb of instrument	This adverb is important. We must believe not merely with our heads, but with our hearts.	
that you believe	Present tense active verb	The subject of the clause ("you") does the action of believing, in contrast to the passive verb that follows. Notice that it is present tense. You *believe* rather than *believed*. The verb tells us that the action is happening now; it did not happen in the past and stop.	
and	Conjunction	The "and" in between two verbs that are not in parallel form is significant in this case because it means that, at the same moment that we believe, we are also justified.	9 4 6
are justified	Present passive verb	This verb is passive. The doer of the action is God (a divine passive). God justifies us; we cannot justify ourselves. It is interesting that this verb is also present tense (present passive). The text does not say "were justified" as an action that happened and finished in the past. It also does not say "will be justified" in the future. Rather, we "are justified" in the present.	
and	Conjunction	The conjunction is joining two related ideas. Notice also that the two related ideas are in parallel form.	6 3
it is with your mouth that you confess and are saved	Extraposed sentence	This extraposed sentence could be rewritten as "you confess with your mouth and are saved." Having it extraposed gives emphasis to the adverb of instrument "with your mouth."	3
it is	Placeholder subject	The "it" is just a placeholder. The logical subject comes after the verb in an extraposed sentence.	
with your mouth	Adverb of instrument	This adverb is important. We must confess with our mouths.	
that you confess	Subject Present tense active verb	The subject of the clause ("you") does the action of confessing. Notice that it is again present tense. You *confess* rather than *confessed*.	9 2 4 6
and	Conjunction	The "and" in between two verbs that are not parallel is significant in this case again because it means that, at the same moment that we confess, we are also saved.	
are saved	Present passive verb	This verb is present passive. The doer of the action is God (a divine passive). God saves us (present tense, not past or future); we cannot save ourselves.	

Sentence 3: *As the Scripture says, "Anyone who trusts in him will never be put to shame."*

Word or Phrase	Type of Structure	Notes	Chapter with Concept
as the Scripture	Sentence introducer	This introductory phrase gives us background information. The author begins by pointing out that he is quoting Scripture.	6 4
says	Present tense	Even words that were written a long time ago are referred to in present tense. This is significant. The present tense shows us that the Scriptures continue to speak.	
anyone	Indefinite pronoun	This pronoun opens the opportunity to any person. This idea continues into the next verses in the form of "all" and "everyone."	
who trusts in him	Restrictive relative clause to head "anyone"	The relative clause is restrictive, which means that it is a necessary specification to "anyone."	
	Present tense (active)	The person must take action and trust.	5 8 4 6 9 7
	Adverb of destination with personal pronoun "him"	Shows where the trust is to be placed. The "him" refers to Jesus. See sentence 1.	
never	Adverb of frequency ("never")	Answers the question "how often" while making the verb phrase negative.	
will [never] be put to shame	Future passive tense followed by adjective	The "will" indicates that this is a possible future condition. (In this case, however, the person who trusts in Jesus will never be shamed. It is a future negative.)	

Sentence 4: *For there is no difference between Jew and Gentile—the same Lord is Lord of all and richly blesses all who call on him, for, "Everyone who calls on the name of the Lord will be saved."*

Word or Phrase	Type of Structure	Notes	Chapter with Concept
for	Conjunction	This sentence completes the thought from the sentence or idea that preceded it.	6
there	Extraposed sentence	"There" is acting as a placeholder for the subject of the sentence.	
is	Present tense	Present tense shows us that this is true today.	3 4 5 7
no difference	Determiner "no"	The determiner "no" creates a negative.	
between Jew and Gentile	Adjective phrase after head ("difference")	The adjectival phrase "between Jew and Gentile" describes the type of "difference."	

Word or Phrase	Type of Structure	Notes	Chapter with Concept
the same Lord	Adjective	We don't need the adjective "same" to identify "Lord," but using this adjective reinforces the contrast between Jew and Gentile. They are different, but God is "the same Lord."	7 2 5
is	Linking verb	This can often be thought of as an equal sign. The same Lord = Lord of all.	
Lord of all	Predicate nominative with adjective phrase ("of all")	This noun phrase renames the same Lord in the subject. The adjective phrase in the predicate nominative is important to describe Lord because it is inclusive.	
and	Coordinating conjunction	An "and" joins related and equal ideas.	6
[*the same Lord*]	Ellipsis	Remember the subject: *the same Lord.*	3 9 2 4 5 8 6
richly	Adverb of extent	It isn't enough to be simply blessed; we can be assured that we'll be "richly" blessed.	
blesses	Present tense transitive verb with direct object	The verb is transitive; it has direct objects ("all who call on him") who receive the action of the verb, the blessing.	
all who call on him	Restrictive relative clause attached to head "all"	The restrictive adjectival clause narrows the scope of those who will be blessed. This sentence does NOT say that the Lord richly blesses ALL.	
on him	Personal pronoun in adverb of recipient ("on him")	The antecedent (referent) of the pronoun is "the same Lord." The adverb of recipient tells us that the Lord ("him") receives our call.	
for	Conjunction	This conjunction shows that the idea continues from the preceding point.	6
everyone	Pronoun	"Everyone" is an inclusive pronoun.	5 8 2 4
who calls on the name of the Lord	Restrictive relative clause attached to head "everyone"	Again, the restrictive nature of the relative clause is vital to the meaning. The relative clause restricts the meaning of those who will be saved to those who call on the name of the Lord. The restrictive relative clause clearly says that not everyone will be saved, but only everyone who calls on the name of the Lord.	
the name of the Lord	Direct object of verb "calls on"	The direct object tells us that the Lord receives our call.	
will be saved	Passive verb with meaning of future	This is another example of the divine passive. Everyone who calls on the Lord will be saved by God, not by himself or herself. Also, the future condition given by "will" is important because it includes us and people who are yet to be born.	

Sentences 5-8: *How, then, can they call on the one they have not believed in? And how can they believe in the one of whom they have not heard? And how can they hear without someone preaching to them? And how can they preach unless they are sent?*

Word or Phrase	Type of Structure	Notes	Chapter with Concept
entire passage	Questions	This set of questions is rhetorical. The answer is implied. In this case, the answer to each of the questions is the same: they cannot.	3
how,	Substitution for adverb	It begins the question, but if put in regular sentence form, it would go at the end of the sentence as follows: "They can call on the one they have not believed in how?"	
then,	Adverbial conjunction	In this case, "then" signals the next part of Paul's argument. Since everyone who calls on the name of the Lord will be saved, then how…	
they	Personal pronoun	"They" refers to "all" and "everyone" earlier.	
can [they] call on	Conditional transitive verb (with verb particle)	The auxiliary verb "can" suggests that the action is possible to do. A transitive verb requires a direct object. They must call on someone.	9 6 4 2 5 8
the one [whom] they have not believed in?	Direct object with restrictive relative clause attached to head "the one"	This head ("the one") offers an interesting contrast to the all-inclusive pronouns in the rest of the passage. Notice the definite determiner "the." It is not *one*, but ***the one***.	
have not believed in	Present perfect verb (with verb particle)	The present perfect construction means that the action began in the past and continues through the present.	
not	Negative auxiliary to the verb	This little word is crucial to the passage, explaining the predicament of those who try to call on God without believing.	
and	Conjunction	This conjunction joins all the questions. At this point, we can also see the parallelism that shows the similarity in the questions ("how can they …")	6 3
how can they	Personal pronoun	See the commentary in the section above. Much of it applies here as well.	
can believe in	Conditional transitive verb (with verb particle)	The verb particle ("in") reminds us that belief is always placed in someone or something; it never just exists.	9 6 4 2 5 8
the one of whom they have not heard	Direct object with restrictive relative clause attached to head "the one"	Again, the restrictive relative clause provides the important information that they have not heard of the one in whom they are to believe.	
have not heard	Present perfect verb	The present perfect tense indicates that the condition of not hearing continues into the present.	

Word or Phrase	Type of Structure	Notes	Chapter with Concept
and how can they hear	Personal pronoun Conditional verb	See comments above for these.	
without someone preaching to them	Adverb clause of condition	This adverb clause of condition is important to Paul's logic. Someone needs to preach before anyone will hear.	6 4 9
someone	Indefinite pronoun head	This "someone" is ambiguous (indefinite), rather than a specific person. All we know about "someone" is found in the attached adjectival modifier ("preaching to them").	5 7 8
preaching to them	Restrictive adjectival modifier attached to head "someone"		
and how can they preach	Personal pronoun Conditional verb	This time "they" refers to "someone preaching to them." Other structures parallel those above.	6 5
unless they are sent	Adverb of condition	This clause gives the necessary condition for preaching; they must be sent.	4 9
are sent	Passive verb	Someone else is doing the sending.	

Sentence 9: *As it is written, "How beautiful are the feet of those who bring good news!"*

Word or Phrase	Type of Structure	Notes	Chapter with Concept
as it is written	Sentence introducer	This introductory phrase gives us background information. This has been written in Scripture.	
it	Pronoun	This "it" refers to the quote that follows.	6 5
is written	Passive verb	The passive requires a doer of the action. In this context, we can assume that God has done the writing.	4
how beautiful are the feet of those who bring good news	Inverted sentence	Normally, the sentence would read, "The feet of those who bring good news are how beautiful!" The inversion gives emphasis to the predicate adjective "how beautiful."	3
how beautiful	Predicate adjective with qualifier	"How" is a qualifier modifying "beautiful."	
are the feet	Linking verb	A linking verb connects the subject with the predicate adjective. In this case, the usual order has been reversed.	2 3
[the feet] of those	Adjectival phrase	The feet belong to specific people.	7 8
who bring good news	Restrictive relative clause, describing the head "those"	The restrictive clause identifying the demonstrative pronoun "those" shows us that not all feet are beautiful, only the ones of those who bring good news.	5 4
bring good news	Transitive verb with direct object "good news"	The people bring something – good news! Also notice the present tense (rather than past or future).	

Therefore, in this passage, Paul explains how we must be saved and under what condition others can be saved. He explains why we need to preach the gospel and finishes by praising those who bring it.

Comparison between Different Versions

Translations between languages are never a one-to-one correspondence. Different languages use different means of communicating the same concepts, often through different grammatical structures. The many versions of the Scriptures differ in how much they will try to parallel the original Greek or Hebrew text in an English construction. Because the three languages are completely different and use different means, translators need to strike a balance between creating a proper, correct English translation and maintaining a close integrity to the text. Ultimately, however, any translation will never be exactly like the original language. This book is not meant to help you pick a version of the Bible, but instead to provide you with tools so that you can better understand English as you read your Bible.

The following are various examples of how different versions treat the same verses.

Luke 1:51

In this passage we will look at the different ways the passages describe the people that God has scattered.

NIV: *He has performed mighty deeds with his arm; he has scattered those **who are proud in their inmost thoughts**.*
  - This version uses a restrictive relative clause and an adjectival completer phrase.

NLT: *His mighty arm has done tremendous things! He has scattered the **proud and haughty** ones.*
  - This version uses two single word adjectives with a conjunction.

NCV: *He has done mighty deeds by his power. He has scattered the people **who are proud and think great things about themselves**.*
  - This version uses a compound relative clause and an adjectival prepositional phrase.

HCSB: *He has done a mighty deed with His arm; He has scattered the proud **because of the thoughts of their hearts**.*
  - This version is different from the others since it uses an adverbial phrase of reason to answer "why" the Lord scattered the proud. It also has an adjectival prepositional phrase.

NASB: *He has done mighty deeds with His arm; He has scattered those **who were proud in the thoughts of their heart**.*
  - Another relative clause, a completer phrase, and an adjectival prepositional phrase are used by this version.

ESV: *He has shown strength with his arm; he has scattered the proud **in the thoughts of their hearts**.*
  - This version simply uses an adjective with a completer to describe the proud.

NKJV: *He has shown strength with His arm; He has scattered the proud **in the imagination of their hearts**.*
  - Similar to the ESV, this uses an adjectival phrase with a completer.

The difference between the versions is often whether they will use a relative clause to describe these people or adjectival phrases, sometimes with completers. However, both relative clauses and adjectival phrases function as adjectives, so the variety in the versions does not cause a problem.

Ephesians 2:4

Although this verse is not a complete sentence, it provides some interesting insight about the differences between English versions.

NIV: *But because of his great love for us, God, who is rich in mercy*
- This version begins with an adverbial prepositional phrase of reason and describes God using a nonrestrictive relative clause.

NLT: *But God is so rich in mercy, and he loved us so much*
- Here, what was a dependant clause in the previous version has been made into two independent clauses joined by a conjunction. There is no cause and effect relationship involved.

NCV: *But God's mercy is great, and he loved us very much.*
- In a similar manner, this version creates two independent clauses.

HCSB: *But God, who is abundant in mercy, because of His great love that He had for us,*
- This version has a nonrestrictive relative clause and an adverbial phrase of reason, in which is imbedded a second relative clause describing "His great love." This is similar to NIV.

NASB: *But God, being rich in mercy, because of His great love with which He loved us*
- This version only has one relative clause, again describing God's love and imbedded within the adverb clause of reason. "Being rich in mercy" is an adjectival active participial phrase (see Chapter 7).

ESV: *But God, being rich in mercy, because of the great love with which he loved us,*
- The ESV is very similar to the NASB and includes all the same elements.

NKJV: *But God, who is rich in mercy, because of His great love with which He loved us*
- Here, the NKJV uses two relative clauses, one to describe God and one to describe his love, as well as an adverbial phrase of reason.

There appear to be three main options for the translators of this verse. They could change the subordinate clause into an independent one, use one relative clause and an adverbial phrase of reason, or have two relative clauses and the adverb of reason. Without the adverb of reason, the NLT and the NCV change the meaning somewhat, but all of them convey the greatness of God's love and his attribute of mercy.

Psalm 7:9
Look at how this passage describes the God who is capable of knowing our thoughts and hearts.

NIV: *O righteous God, who searches minds and hearts, bring to an end the violence of the wicked and make the righteous secure.*
- This version uses a relative clause to describe God's quality of searching minds and hearts.

NLT: *End the evil of those who are wicked, and defend the righteous. For you look deep within the mind and heart, O righteous God.*
- Here, that same quality is described through a direct statement in a subject and predicate.

NCV: *God, you do what is right. You know our thoughts and feelings. Stop those wicked actions done by evil people, and help those who do what is right.*
- Phrased even more differently, the verbs in the first two sentences are changed, and these sentences are declarative, direct statements. The last sentence has two imperatives or requests.

HCSB: *Let the evil of the wicked come to an end, but establish the righteous. The One who examines the thoughts and emotions is a righteous God.*
- Similar to the NIV, the HCSB uses a relative clause to describe God. Notice, however, that the position in the verse is opposite, and that it is broken into two sentences rather than one.

NASB: *O let the evil of the wicked come to an end, but establish the righteous; for the righteous God tries the hearts and minds.*
- Again, a direct statement is made here, but the two sentences are joined with a semicolon.

ESV: *Oh, let the evil of the wicked come to an end, and may you establish the righteous—you who test the minds and hearts, O righteous God!*

- In this version, the phrase directly addresses God, using a relative clause to describe the testing.

NKJV: *Oh, let the wickedness of the wicked come to an end, but establish the just; for the righteous God tests the hearts and minds.*

- Paralleling the construction of the NASB, the NKJV uses a direct statement, joined to the previous one with a semicolon.

This comparison shows a stronger variation between the versions as they attempt to convey the awesomeness of a righteous God who is able to look and know our hearts and thoughts.

As you can see, the different versions often are able to convey the same meaning, with perhaps different shades or nuances, depending on their construction. With the tools in this book, you will be able to analyze critically these differences in your own Bible study.

Where do we go from here?

It is a great responsibility to study the Word of God. The instructions in 2 Timothy 2:15 are clear: *"Be diligent to present yourself approved to God as a workman who does not need to be ashamed, accurately handling the word of truth"* (NIV). Furthermore, Hebrews 4:12 describes this Word of truth: *"For the word of God is living and active, sharper than any two-edged sword, piercing to the division of soul and of spirit, of joints and of marrow, and discerning the thoughts and intentions of the heart"* (ESV).

The goal of this book is to present you with some of the tools that you need in order to study the Bible more effectively. It is important to remember, however, that using these tools does not ensure that you will discover truth. Good exegesis and maintaining a high respect for the context and the text are absolutely imperative when studying the Word of God. Always be sure to approach the text with humility, seeking to learn what it has to teach you.

May you be blessed in your biblical study as you use these tools of English grammar.

Index

absolute, 50–51, 53, 54
adjectival appositive, 59
adjective, 3, 4, 5, 8, 9, 10, 11, 14, 25, 34, 40, 55, 56, 57, 58, 59, 60, 62, 63, 64, 65, 66, 68, 69, 73, 79, 89, 92, 93, 94, 95, 96, 97, 100, 101, 103, 104, 105
adverb, 3, 8, 9, 10, 11, 12, 13, 14, 60, 75, 76, 77, 78, 79, 80, 81, 82, 83, 84, 85, 86, 87, 88, 89, 90, 91, 92, 93, 94, 95, 96, 97, 98, 99, 100, 101, 102, 103, 104, 105
   adverb question, 10, 75–76
antecedent, 43, 44, 52, 53, 67, 101
command, 9, 25, 26, 27, 28, 31, 32, 50, 52, 62, 79, 84
conjunction, 45–50, 53, 54, 77, 90, 91, 93, 96, 97, 98, 99, 100, 101, 102, 104, 105
   adverbial conjunction, 49–50
   coordinating conjunction, 45–48, 49, 50, 53, 54, 58, 90, 91, 93, 94
   subordinating conjunction, 48–49, 77, 92, 97
determiner, 34–35, 41, 42, 43, 92, 93, 95, 102
direct object, 3, 6, 7, 8, 9, 10, 11, 12, 19, 20, 21, 31, 33, 91, 93, 95, 96, 97, 98, 101, 102, 103
divine passive, 29, 30, 31, 96, 97, 98, 99, 101
Edited American English, 1, 2, 13, 14, 15, 16, 20, 25, 30, 37, 47, 60, 66, 71, 98
ellipsis, 10, 12, 18–19, 21, 45, 57, 61, 70, 91, 96, 101
extraposed sentence, 15–16, 19, 20, 21, 22, 31, 63, 64, 98, 99
gerund phrase, 37, 38
head, 37, 38, 39, 40, 41, 42, 50, 58, 59, 60, 61, 62, 63, 64, 65, 66, 67, 68, 69, 70, 71, 72, 73, 74, 90, 91, 94, 95, 96, 97, 100, 101, 102, 103
indirect object, 7, 10, 33, 91
infinitive phrase, 37, 38, 41, 56, 58, 60, 62, 63, 77, 96
intensifier, 40, 41
inverted sentence, 4, 13–15, 16, 19, 20, 30, 44, 55, 80, 85
   poetic inversion, 14, 55
metaphor, 5, 6, 36, 41, 42, 81, 87, 95
nominal, 3, 6, 8, 33, 37, 63, 73
nonrestrictive modifier, 66, 67, 68, 69, 73, 74, 95, 105
noun, 3, 4, 6, 8, 33, 34, 35, 37, 38, 40, 41, 50, 53, 55, 58, 59, 60, 61, 62, 63, 64, 65, 77, 90, 92, 94, 95, 97, 101
noun appositive, 37–40, 40, 41, 42, 50, 61, 64, 68, 94, 97
noun clause, 37, 38
noun of direct address, 51–52, 53, 89, 97
parallelism, 16–18, 21, 90, 91, 93, 98, 99, 102, 103
participial phrase, 61–62, 64, 105

placeholder word, 15, 16, 21, 98, 99, 100
predicate, 3–4, 89, 93, 94, 95, 96, 98, 105
predicate adjective, 3, 4, 5, 6, 8, 9, 31, 55, 56, 57, 58, 59, 63, 64, 70, 90, 93, 103
predicate nominative, 3, 4, 5, 6, 8, 9, 12, 31, 33, 35–37, 41, 42, 68, 94
prepositional phrase, 10, 56, 57, 58, 59, 60, 62, 63, 66, 70, 76, 77, 78, 80, 85, 87, 91, 104, 105
pro-form, 43, 45, 52
pronoun, 19, 20, 21, 33, 34, 40, 41, 42, 43, 44, 45, 52, 53, 54, 55, 60, 61, 65, 67, 69, 71, 89, 90, 91, 92, 94, 95, 96, 97, 100, 101, 102, 103
   demonstrative pronoun, 41, 42, 44–45, 52, 54, 94
   indefinite pronoun, 45, 52
   personal pronoun, 44, 52, 90
   possessive pronoun, 52
   relative pronoun, 60, 61
question, 13, 19, 20, 21, 22, 89, 90, 91, 102
   rhetorical question, 13, 20
referent, 43, 44
relative clause, 20, 42, 60, 61, 62, 64, 65, 66, 67, 68, 69, 70, 71, 72, 73, 74, 90, 91, 92, 95, 100, 101, 102, 103, 104, 105, 106
restrictive modifier, 66, 67, 68, 69, 73, 74, 90, 91, 92, 100, 101, 102, 103, 104
sentence introducer, 25, 52, 53, 100, 103
simile, 5, 6, 57, 58, 63, 68
subject, 3–4, 5, 6, 8, 9, 10, 11, 12, 15, 16, 20, 21, 22, 25, 27, 28, 31, 33, 36, 38, 41, 42, 44, 45, 55, 56, 57, 58, 63, 64, 67, 68, 89, 91, 92, 93, 94, 95, 96, 98, 99, 100, 101, 103, 105
unconventional sentence, 19–20
verb, 3, 4–8
   active verb, 28, 30, 31, 61, 64, 77, 99, 100, 105
   auxiliary verb, 23, 24, 25, 31, 102
   conditional, 25, 28, 31, 32, 98
   emphatic verb, 30, 31, 45
   future, 23, 24, 31, 32, 99, 100, 101
   imperative, 9, 25, 26, 27, 31, 32, 105
   intransitive verb, 8, 89
   linking verb, 4, 5, 4–6, 9, 12, 31, 35, 42, 68, 90, 94, 101, 103
   passive verb, 28, 29, 30, 28–30, 31, 32, 61, 67, 78, 81, 92, 96, 98, 99, 100, 101, 103
   past tense, 23, 24, 31, 32, 99
   perfect, 24, 25, 30, 31, 102
   present tense, 23, 24, 30, 31, 99, 100, 101, 102
   progressive tense, 23, 24, 30, 31
   transitive verb, 6–8, 9, 10, 11, 12, 93, 95, 96, 97, 98, 101, 102, 103
   verb particle, 23

vocative, 51–52